"Your little work is truly a [...] the doctrine of the Fathers. I have read it with profit and consolation, and I rejoice in the consolation that it will bring to souls wanting instruction on this point."

—Louis Édouard François Desiré Pie
Cardinal Bishop of Poitiers, France

"This work deserves a distinguished place in all Christian libraries and should be on the table of every pious family that faithfully preserves and celebrates the memory of its deceased members."

—*Vienne Post*
November 6, 1862

"Your charming work is admirably adapted to console many poor, afflicted souls who, having enjoyed here below the happiness of loving their dear ones, find difficulty in conceiving that they can be happy far away from them. Your book is a good work—a true act of charity."

—André-Jean-Marie Hamon
Priest of St. Sulpice, France

"For a long time, I have wished that such a book should be given to the public."

—Félix Antoine Philibert Dupanloup
Bishop of Orléans, France

In Heaven We'll Meet Again

François René Blot, S.J.

In Heaven
We'll Meet Again

The Saints and Scripture
on Our Heavenly Reunion

SOPHIA INSTITUTE PRESS
Manchester, New Hampshire

Contents

In Heaven We'll Meet Again

EDITOR'S NOTE: Published in 1863 as a translation from an earlier French edition, this book at times cites as the source of its information books of which there is no present record. Occasionally, it inaccurately cites texts and passages. We have attempted to remedy these occasional deficiencies, but where we have failed, we have omitted the author's unverifiable attribution rather than risk misleading the reader.

From the Preface to the Seventh Edition

The success of this book has itself given great joy to the sensitive soul of the person who first asked us for these *Letters of Consolation*. She writes:

I am certainly indebted to you for much consolation and many good desires. You are always kind enough to let me hear of the success of the work *In Heaven We'll Meet Again*. For this I thank you with all my heart. When I think that my sighs and my tears have drawn this book from your heart, I can only admire Divine Providence, which from a grain of mustard seed, has produced a tree under whose shadow the souls of the afflicted repose.

Alas! In her life, death has again lifted his sword, again snatching from this poor mother a beloved daughter. But grace lent her some resemblance to Mary, by her religious resignation:

> I consecrated myself by a vow to our good Mother at the most terrible moment of my grief, and she came to my help. Although I did not remain standing, like her, at the foot of the Cross, I seated myself there, and left it not. It was she who obtained for me grace to do so.

May all mothers from whom death tears a child also invoke and imitate her who beheld her only Son crucified! May all those who read this little work have recourse to the Comforter of the Afflicted and at least seat themselves at the foot of the Cross, if there they cannot stand!

—François René Blot, S.J.
Paris, May 29, 1863

Letter 1

State of the Question

M adam,
Death has cruelly stricken around you the persons
you loved most. Your grief is extreme, and it is lawful, even
though you feel no doubt of their eternal salvation. Why
should you be forbidden to mourn your nearest and dearest
who sleep in the Lord, provided that, following the counsel
of the Apostle, you be not sorrowful even as others who
have no hope? (1 Thess. 4:12).[1]

St. Augustine (354-430) comments on these words:

It is natural to grieve at the death of those who are
dear to us, since death is abhorrent to nature, and
faith teaches us that it is one of the chastisements
of sin. Sorrow is a necessity when those whom we

[1] RSV = 1 Thess. 4:13.

love depart from us by dying. For, although we know that they have not departed from us forever (as if we were to remain always on earth), but that they have preceded us by a little (because we are destined soon to follow them), nevertheless how shall death, taking possession of our friend, not afflict our natural affection? Let it then be permitted to loving hearts to sorrow for the death of their beloved, provided that there be a remedy for this grief, a consolation for these tears, in the joy of which faith gives us some foretaste, in rendering us confident of the fate of our dear deceased, who go only a little before us, and pass into a better life.[2]

St. Paulinus, bishop of Nola, consoled Pammachius, who had lost his wife, Paulina, daughter of St. Paula, and sister of St. Eustochium. The virtuous husband shed tears as abundantly as he dispensed alms. What will his friend do? Will he blame him for these tears? He will, on the contrary, commend him and gather from Scripture all the examples of holy tears shed at the death of a cherished friend. He will then add:

---

[2] St. Augustine, Sermon 172, no. 12.

State of the Question

Why condemn the mourning of holy mortals? Did
not Jesus Himself weep for Lazarus, whom He loved?
Did He not deign to commiserate our unhappiness
so far as to shed tears over one that was dead? Did
He not, humbling Himself to the level of human
infirmity, weep for him whom He was about to raise
to life by means of His divine virtue? It is for this, O
my brother, that your tears are pious and holy; for
a similar affection causes them to flow; and if you
weep for a worthy and chaste companion, it is not
that you have doubts of the resurrection, but that
your love has its regrets and its desires.[3]

In the presence of those who reproach you with your
tears, open the Gospel, and, for your answer, point to the
words of St. John, "And Jesus wept," and again these, "And
he troubled himself" (cf. John 11:33, 35).

It was the will of Jesus to deny Himself that solace to
be found in a *calm* affliction; it was His will to be *troubled*.
His divine nature permitted Him so to be, only inasmuch
as He Himself concurred in this trouble; and that He did
this the Gospel tells us. After such an example, let us no

[3] St. Paulinus, Epistle 13, nos. 4, 5.

Detail from Jesus Wept, *by James Tissot*

longer attribute to our imperfection the tears wrung from us by affliction, or the trouble into which it casts us — *Jesus wept, Jesus was troubled.*

That this trouble does not degenerate into uneasiness is all that is requisite to preserve its resemblance to that of Jesus.

God forbid that I should disapprove the mourn-ing of a husband, who, after having raised his eyes to heaven, there to see his spouse crowned with immortality, feels them fill with tears as, turning them down to earth again, he no longer finds his beloved companion by his side! The sentiment that causes us to regret the person whose companionship formed our happiness cannot be blamable when it is not the only source of the tears that we give to our loss. This desire to enjoy the society of those we love is so natural to man that God offers him its gratification as the eternal reward of his fidelity to the divine love during life.[4]

Fully to enjoy what we have loved, religiously, on earth, is then heaven for us. To enjoy God constitutes the primary beatitude; to enjoy creatures, the secondary beatitude.

This enjoyment of the created being, without ceasing to be secondary, becomes itself a sweet consolation to our hearts from the moment that death snatches from us those whom we loved the most, and God, to moderate our grief, sends us the hope of beholding them once more, of recognizing them, of loving them in particular again in heaven, and also of receiving from them the proofs of

[4] Louis Provano de Collegno, *The Consolations of Religion at the Death of Those Who Are Dear to Us*, Letter 1.

a special affection. How often has not this hope been a balsam to your wounds, a solace to your grief!

But there are several, even of those whose lips should keep knowledge and whose hearts should be the depository of the law (Mal. 2:7), who have ventured to tell you that in the other world, in paradise even, friends do not recognize one another. Moreover, they have condemned, as an imperfection, your ardent desire to possess in heaven, besides the Creator, certain tenderly cherished creatures — your husband and your children. In fine, they make people believe that Christian perfection, and, still more, religious life, dries up, in the heart of man, the source of sensibility, to leave it withered and cold toward parents, brothers, sisters, and friends. "In heaven all are forgotten in God," they say. "Is not God sufficient for you? The saints loved God alone."

These are the three errors that, in writing to you, I purpose to combat.

Those who maintain them follow, perhaps without knowing it, in the track of the Quietists and the Jansenists beneath the standards of antireligious philosophism. In the desire to enjoy God Himself, Quietism embraced a violation of pure love and a disinterestedness. Jansenism — polished as a mirror, but also as cold — communicated its hardness and its inflexibility to a religion of love. The unbelieving philosophers profited by these tendencies to attack the Church and to throw discredit on the clergy. A learned religious of the order of Saint Dominic, discussing, in the eighteenth century, the subject of which I am now treating, drew attention to this maneuver of impiety. While everything in our religion tends to render her most amiable and most consoling, a deceptive philosophism attributes to her dark and desperate doctrines that rob her of all that power of attraction that she needs in order to lead souls to love and follow Jesus Christ.[5]

Do you want an example? Rousseau makes a dying person say:

> A hundred times I have taken more pleasure in performing a good action by imagining my mother present, reading the heart of her daughter, and applauding her. There is something so consoling in still living under the eye of one who was dear to us! It makes such a one only half die to us!

But what sentiments does Rousseau—this enemy of all revealed religion, Catholic or Protestant—lend to the

---

[5] P. F. Casto Innocente Ansaldi, *Della Speranza e della Consolazione di rivedere i cari nostri nell'altra vita*, chap. 10.

minister who approaches to console and fortify the sick?
Read:

> Although the pastor replied to all with great gen-
> tleness and moderation, and even affected not to
> contradict her in anything, lest his silence on other
> points should be taken for consent, he did not fail
> to show himself the priest, for one moment at least,
> and to state an opposite doctrine on the other life.
> He said that the immensity, the glory, and the attri-
> butes of God would be the only objects that would
> occupy the souls of the blessed; that this sublime
> contemplation would efface every other remem-
> brance; that we should not see or recognize each
> other, even in heaven; and that in God's entranc-
> ing presence we should think no more of anything
> earthly.[6]

Let whoever propagates this gloomy doctrine, be he
sincere minister of religion or pious layman, see, now, what
cause he serves, in what ranks he is found!

To prove to you its falsity, I will, madam, pass in review
before you a great number of those authors who, from

---

[6] J.J. Rousseau, *Julie*, 6, Letter 2.

their antiquity, their knowledge, their orthodoxy, and their sanctity, have been called the Fathers and Doctors of the Church. They will all let you penetrate into their hearts. It will be as agreeable as it will be useful to you to see how sensible they always were to the hope of recognizing and loving again, after death, those whom they had known and loved during life.

Lazarus and the Rich Man, *by James Lansveld*

Letter 2

In Heaven All Know Each Other

Madam,
    All the blessed, admitted into heaven, know each other perfectly, even before the general resurrection. This is proved by Scripture as well as by tradition.

I shall confine myself to quoting the New Testament to you; I shall content myself, too, with the parable of the rich man, and with some words that have reference to the Last Judgment.

This parable is so fine that I cannot resist the pleasure of placing some of its leading points before you.

> There was a certain rich man who was clothed in purple and fine linen, and feasted sumptuously every day; and there was a certain beggar named Lazarus who lay at his gate, full of sores, desiring to be filled with the crumbs that fell from the rich man's

table—but none were given to him; moreover, the dogs came and licked his sores. And it came to pass that the beggar died, and was carried by the angels into Abraham's bosom; and the rich man also died, and he was buried in hell. And, when he was in torments, lifting up his eyes, he saw Abraham afar off and Lazarus in his bosom, and he cried and said: "Father, Abraham, have mercy on me, and send Lazarus that he may dip the tip of his finger in water, and cool my tongue, for I am tormented in this flame."

And Abraham said to him: "Son, remember that thou didst receive good things in thy lifetime, and likewise Lazarus evil things; but now he is comforted, and thou art tormented. . . .

And the rich man said: "Father, I beseech thee that thou wouldst send him to my father's house, for I have five brethren, that he may testify unto them, lest they come also in this place of torment." (Luke 16:19-31)

This is what made St. Irenaeus, when combating heretics in the beginning of the third century, write:

The Lord has revealed to us that in another life souls are mindful of the actions which they performed in

In Heaven All Know Each Other

St. Irenaeus

this. Does He not teach us this truth in the history of the bad rich man and of Lazarus? For Abraham knows what relates both to one and to the other. Souls continue, then, to know one another, and to remember those things which are here below.[7]

In the eighth century, the Venerable Bede put this question to himself: "Do the good know each other in the

---

[7] Irenaeus, *Against Heresies*, bk. 2, chap. 34, no. 1.

kingdom of heaven, and do the bad know the bad in hell?"
He answered in the affirmative:

> I see a proof of it, clearer than day, in the parable of
> the bad rich man. Does not our Lord there openly
> declare that the good know each other, and the
> wicked also? For if Abraham did not know Lazarus,
> how could he speak of his past misfortunes to the
> bad rich man who is in the midst of torments? And
> how could this rich man not know those who are
> present, since he is mindful to pray for those who
> are absent? We see, besides, that the good know
> the wicked, and the wicked the good. In fact, the
> rich man is known to Abraham; and Lazarus, in the
> ranks of the elect, is recognized by the rich man,
> who is among the number of the reprobate.
>
> This knowledge fills up the measure of what
> each shall receive; it causes the just to rejoice the
> more, because they see those they have loved rejoice
> with them; it makes the wicked suffer not only their
> own pains, but also in some sort the pains of others,
> since they are tormented in company with those
> whom they loved in this world to the exclusion
> of God. There is, even for the blessed, something

more admirable still. Beyond the recognition of those whom they have known in this world they recognize also, as if they had seen them and previously known them, the good whom they never saw. For of what can they be ignorant in heaven, since all there behold, in the plenitude of light, the God who knows all?[8]

On the Last Judgment, we have these words of Jesus Christ to his disciples: "Amen, I say to you, that you who have followed me in the regeneration, when the Son of Man shall sit in the seat of his majesty, you also shall sit on twelve seats judging the twelve tribes of Israel" (Matt. 19:28).

We have these words of St. Paul to the Corinthians: "Know you not that the saints shall judge this world? Know you not that we shall judge angels?" (1 Cor. 6:2, 3).

Such is the basis of the argument of St. Theodore Studites (d. 826), in a discourse that he composed at the end of the eighth or the commencement of the ninth century, to refute the error that we are here combating. He said:

Some deceive their hearers by maintaining that the men who rise again will not recognize each other

---

[8] Venerable Bede, *Aliquot quaestionum liber*, q. 12.

when the Son of God comes to judge us all. How, they exclaim, when from perishable we become incorruptible and immortal — when there will no longer be Greek or Jew, barbarian or Scythian, slave or freeman, husband or wife — when we shall all be as spirits, how could we recognize each other?

Let us, in the first place, reply that that which is impossible to man is possible to God; otherwise, blinded by human reasons, we should even disbelieve the resurrection. How, in fact, can a body already in a state of corruption — perhaps devoured by wild beasts, by birds, or by fishes, themselves devoured by others — and that in several ways and at various times successively, be reunited or gathered together on the last day? It will be thus, however, and the hidden power of God will reunite all its scattered parts and raise it up. Then each soul will recognize the body in which it lived.

But will every soul recognize also the body of its neighbor? We cannot doubt it, unless, at the same time, we doubt the general judgment. For no one can be summoned to judgment without being known, and a person must be known to be judged, according to this expression of Scripture: "I will reprove thee and set [thy own transgressions] before thy face" (Ps. 49:21 [RSV = Ps. 50:21]).

The value of this reasoning depends upon the following distinction: in the private judgment, we are judged by God alone, but in the general judgment we shall be, in some measure, judged by one another. Whilst the former will manifest the justice of God only to the soul that is judged, the latter will make it evident to every creature. Therefore, all await that great day for "the revelation of the sons of God" (Rom. 8:19), which will alter all the estimations of men.

The saint continues in these terms:

This is why, if we do not recognize one another, we shall not be judged; if we are not judged, we shall not be rewarded or punished for that which we shall have done and suffered while we were of the number of the living. If the apostles are not to recognize those whom they will judge, will they see the accomplishment of this promise of the Lord: "You shall sit on twelve seats, judging the twelve tribes of Israel" (Matt. 19:28)? If he is not to recognize them in the kingdom of heaven, will the blessed

Job be able to receive twice as many children (Job 42:10-13)? For here below he received only a part, and in order that the promise made to him may be fully accomplished, is it not a necessity that he should receive the remainder in the life to come? Besides, from these words: "No brother can redeem, nor shall man redeem" (Ps. 48:8 [RSV = Ps. 49:7]), does not the holy king David suppose a brother to know his brother?

From all quarters we can collect arguments and authorities against those who assert that we do not recognize one another in heaven—a senseless assertion, whose impiety may be compared to the fables of Origen. For us, my brethren, let us believe still and ever that we shall rise again, we shall be incorruptible, and that we shall know one another, as our first parents knew each other in the earthly paradise, before the existence of sin, when they were yet exempt from all corruption. Yes, it *must* be believed—the brother will know his brother, the father his children, the wife her husband, the friend his friend. I will even add, the religious will know the religious, the confessor will know the confessor, the martyr his fellow soldier, the apostle his colleague in the apostleship—we shall all know one another, in order that the habitation of all in God may be rendered more joyous by this blessing, added to so many others—the blessing of mutual recognition![9]

The light thrown by Catholic tradition upon this subject is so vivid and constant that it dissipates all the clouds of sophistry and prejudice.

The testimonies from tradition may be divided into two classes—those that simply affirm the fact and those that draw consolation from it.

Among the works commonly attributed to St. Athanasius (c. 297-373), that pure glory of the fourth century, is one that has for its title *Necessary Questions of Which No Christian Should Be Ignorant*. Now, in reply to the twenty-second question we read, "To the souls of the just in heaven God grants a great gift, which is mutual recognition."[10]

In the seventh century Pope St. Gregory the Great (c. 540-604), after having related that a religious saw, when dying, the prophets come toward him, and that he addressed them by their names, added: "This example makes us clearly understand how great will be the knowledge

[9] St. Theodore Studites, *Catechetical Sermons*, no. 22.
[10] *Quaestiones ad Antiochum principem*, q. 22.

Pope St. Gregory the Great, *by Antonello da Messina*

which we shall have of one another in the incorruptible life of heaven, since this religious, though still in a corruptible flesh, seemed to recognize the holy prophets, whom, however, he had never seen."[11]

The most illustrious of the abbots of Clairvaux, St. Bernard (1090-1153), also said in the twelfth century: "The

[11] St. Gregory the Great, *Dialogues*, bk. 4, chap. 34.

blessed are united among themselves by a charity which is so much the greater as they are the nearer to God, who is charity. No envy can throw suspicion into their ranks, for there is nothing in one which is concealed from the other; the all-pervading light of truth permits it not."[12]

Were I to question the theologians of modern times, they would unanimously answer in the affirmative. Let one taken from the crowd answer, however, in the name of all:

> The saints see and know each other, as is required by the unity of the kingdom and the unity of the city wherein they reside in the company of the one God; they spontaneously reveal to one another their thoughts and their affections, like the members of one family united by a sincere love. Among their fellow-citizens in heaven, they know even those whom they did not know here below, and their appreciation of noble actions leads them to a more complete knowledge of those who performed them.[13]

[12] St. Bernard, *Sermon 1 for the Dedication of a Church.*

[13] Joannis Laurentii Berti (1696-1766), *De Theologicis disciplinis*, bk. 3, chap. 13.

In Heaven We'll Meet Again

The greatest saints and the greatest men of the Church have not hesitated to have recourse to this truth as to a never-failing spring, whence to draw the pure waters of heavenly consolation with which they solace the afflicted. Who now, therefore, shall dare again to censure this ardent desire, this sweet hope, as an imperfection?

Have you lost a brother or a sister? Console yourself, then, as St. Ambrose (c. 340-397) did:

Brother, since you have preceded me thither, prepare for me a place in that common abode of all, which is for me henceforward the most desirable; and as, here below, everything was in common between us, so in heaven let us remain ignorant of any law of division. I conjure you, keep me not waiting long, so pressing is the desire I experience of rejoining you, help me who am hastening forward, and if I seem to you still to tarry, make me advance; we have never been long separated, but it is you who were in the habit of returning to me. Now that you can no longer return, I will go to you.[14] O my brother!

[14] St. Ambrose, *On the Death of His Brother Satyrus*, bk. 1, nos. 78, 79.

What comfort remains to me but the hope of soon meeting you again? Yes, I comfort myself with the hope that the separation that your departure has caused will not be of long duration, and that by your prayers you will obtain the grace to hasten the coming of him whose regrets for you are so bitter.[15]

Have you lost a son or a daughter? Receive the consolations of a patriarch of Constantinople addressed to a bereft father. This patriarch, Photius, can no more be counted among great men than among saints, as he was the author of the cruel schism that separates the East and the West. Nevertheless, his opinions only prove the better that, on this point, the Greeks and the Latins entertain the same views. Photius says:

If your daughter were to appear to you, and, placing her face, resplendent with glory, against your face and her hand within yours, thus were to speak to you, would it not be to describe the joys of heaven? Then she would add: "Why do you grieve, father? I am in paradise, where felicity is unbounded. You will come someday with my beloved mother, and

[15] Ibid., bk. 2, no. 135.

then you will find that I have not exaggerated the delights of this place, so far will the reality exceed my description. O dearly beloved father, detain me no longer in your arms, but be pleased to permit me to return whither the intensity of my love attracts me." Let us then banish sorrow, for now your daughter is happy in Abraham's bosom. Let us banish sorrow; for it is there that, after a very little time, we shall see her in the ecstasy of joy and delight.[16]

Have you lost your husband? Alas! The mourning garments you so constantly wear show plainly the misfortune that you have sustained; they show, also, how affection has survived the tie broken by death. Seek aid, then, in the consolations so frequently presented by the Church to Christian widows.

St. Jerome (c. 347-420) wrote to a widow:

Regret your Lucinius as a brother; but rejoice that he reigns with Christ. Victorious and secure of his glory, he looks down upon you from the heights of heaven; he is your support in your works and woes,

---

[16] Photius, *Letters*, bk. 3, letter 63.

St. Jerome in His Study, *by Antonio da Fabiano*

and he prepares for you a place by his side, ever preserving for you the same love and charity that, making him forget the names of husband and of wife, compelled him, during his life, to love you as his sister, and to live with you as a brother. For, in the pure union that chastity forms between two hearts, the difference of sex that constitutes marriage is unknown.[17]

St. Augustine wrote to another widow

We have not lost those who leave a world from which we must ourselves depart; but we have sent them before us into that other life, where the better they are known to us, the dearer to us will they become. Your husband knew himself better than you knew him. You saw his face best, but he knew his heart best. When the Lord comes, he will throw light upon everything now enveloped in darkness and make manifest the thoughts of all. Then neighbor will have nothing to hide from neighbor, nor will anyone make a difference between his friend and a stranger—revealing things to the former and concealing them from the latter—since there will then be no strangers. But what will be the nature, what the intensity of the light that will thus illuminate all the secrets buried in the obscurity of our own hearts? Who can say? Who can even conceive it?[18]

[17] St. Jerome to Theodora, *Selected Letters*.
[18] St. Augustine, Letters 92, nos. 1, 2.

In Heaven All Know Each Other

The Triumph of St. Augustine, *by Claudio Coello*

St. John Chrysostom (c. 349-407), in a homily on St. Matthew, said, as if to each of his hearers individually:

Do you wish to behold him whom death has snatched from you? Lead, then, the same life as he in the path of virtue, and you will soon enjoy that blessed sight. But you would wish to see him even here. Ah! Who prevents you? It is both easy and allowable, if you are virtuous; for the hope of future goods is clearer than the possession itself.[19]

This sublime orator found, in his own history, all that could make him sympathize with the sorrows of the wife who has lost her husband. The only son of a young woman, weak alike from her age and her sex, and early left a widow to struggle with the world, he had been the confidant of her tears and of her grief, when he made her as though a second time a widow, by escaping from her love to plunge into solitude. He has himself related to us that the pagan rhetorician Libanius, learning that his mother had been bereft of her husband from the age of twenty, and would never be induced to contract another marriage, exclaimed, turning toward his idolatrous hearers: "O ye gods of Greece! What women there are among those Christians!"

Divine Providence found means to supply Chrysostom with an opportunity of exercising the compassionate feelings of his heart toward the widowed, by consoling another young woman who had passed only five years of her life

[19] St. John Chrysostom, *Homily 31 on Matthew*, nos. 4, 5.

with her husband, Therasius, one of the principal personages of his time. He wrote two treatises for her, and they
are among his most remarkable productions. He says to
her, among other comforting things:

> If you desire to see your husband, if you wish to enjoy
> each other's presence, let your life shine with purity
> like his, and be assured that you will thus enter into
> the same angelic choir that he has already reached.
> You will abide with him, not only during five years,
> as on earth—not only during twenty, a hundred,
> a thousand, two thousand, ten thousand, or many
> more years, but during ages without end. Then you
> will once more find your husband, no longer with
> that corporal beauty with which he was gifted when
> he departed, but with a different splendor—beauty
> of another sort, which will surpass in brilliancy the
> rays of the sun.
>
> If it had been promised to you that the empire
> of the whole earth should be given to your husband,
> on condition that during twenty years you should
> be separated from him, and if, in addition, you had
> received a pledge that after those twenty years, your
> Therasius should be restored to you, adorned with

the diadem and the purple, and you yourself placed in the same rank of honor as he, would you not have resigned yourself to this separation, and easily have preserved continence? You would even have seen in this offer a signal favor, and something worthy of all your desires. Now, therefore, bear with patience the separation which gives your husband the kingdom, not of earth, but of heaven; bear it, that you may find him among the blessed inhabitants of paradise, clad, not with a vesture of gold, but with one of glory and immortality.

This is why, in thinking of the honors that Therasius enjoys in heaven, you must cease to weep and lament. Live as he lived, and even with more perfection. By this means, after having practiced the same virtues, you will be received into the same tabernacles, and you can once more be united to him in the eternal ages, not by the tie of marriage, but by another and a better tie. The first unites bodies only, while the second, more pure, more blissful, and more holy, unites soul to soul.[20]

[20] St. John Chrysostom, *To a Young Widow*, nos. 3, 4.

Letter 3

Heaven Is Love and Light

Madam,

Our faith in any truth solidly established in the Church must not be shaken by one or more objections, the solution of which eludes our observation. Truth is of the Lord, and remaineth forever, says the Scriptures (cf. Ps. 116:2 [RSV = Ps. 117:2]). Objections are from man; time changes them, and the breath of science disperses them.

Nevertheless, it often happens that a truth, clearly demonstrated, does not penetrate deeply into our souls as long as we feel a difficulty about it to which we do not perceive the reply. Sometimes the objection takes possession of our minds to such a degree as to banish the truth from them. This is what has happened to many persons with regard to the truth of which we are treating. Not knowing how to remove the veil formed by some difficulties that

In Heaven We'll Meet Again

Detail from Dante and the Divine Comedy,
by Domenico di Michelino

conceal this consoling truth from them, they have denied
the recognition of souls in heaven. They have acted with
the imprudence of a child, who might say, because unable
to dissipate the mist and clouds, that there was no sun.

All the objections made to you, and transmitted by you
to me, proceed from this source — the want of a sufficiently
grand and just idea of heaven. Many suppose that God

would be inclined to erect the edifice of our greatness on indifference or insensibility, to crown us with glory and to satiate us with felicity in the midst of ignorance and darkness.

To attach oneself to this idea is to prove that one has not read Dante, that prince of Christian poets, who placed his powerful and regulated imagination at the service of faith and who sang in a language and in a country not altogether foreign to your family. I quote him, not to attribute to him an authority that he does not possess, but because he very happily expresses the Catholic thought. He says:

> Heaven is an admirable and angelic temple, whose only limits are love and light—an intellectual light charged with love, the love of real good filled with joy surpassing all sweetness. The state of beatitude is founded on the act of seeing; that of loving comes only in the second instance. And the joy even of the blessed, like that of the angels, is more or less great accordingly as their vision plunges more or less far into the truth where all intellectual effort is at rest.[21]

[21] Dante, *Paradise*, canto 28.

Here, then, is the principle of solution for objections — in heaven, which is less a place than a state, all is light, all is love.

By this light, the elect, who enjoy the clear vision of God, know, besides the wonders of nature and grace, all that belongs to the particular state of each. Thus, pontiffs see what relates to the government of their churches, and kings that which concerns their kingdoms. It is to be supposed that their life is perfect by reason of the assemblage of all goods; and would it be so without this recognition?

We must believe that they see God face-to-face. Why, in this mirror of the Divinity — always faithfully reflecting and ever open to their eyes — why should they not see that which concerns and interests them? The blessed have an infused and actual wisdom that comes to them by means of revelation and illumination, either from God or from the angels and saints higher than themselves in glory. They have also a natural and acquired wisdom, obtained during this life either by theory or by experience, and preserved in heaven. Could they, then, lose in the abode of felicity that acquirement of all others most fit to increase their happiness — the knowledge of the relations and friends whom they possessed here below?

They are ignorant neither of the wants nor of the prayers of their clients in this world. They govern; they direct us; they intercede for us. St. Gregory of Nazianzen (c. 329-390), in ending the eulogium of St. Cyprian (c. 200-258), exclaimed: "Oh! From the heights of heaven look down upon us graciously, govern our speech and our lives, feed this virtuous flock and aid its pastor."[22]

In the second book of Maccabees (15:12, 16) we see Onias and Jeremias, already dead, interested in the fate of the Jews, praying for their deliverance, and giving to Judas the sword to insure the victory. In Revelation 5:8 we see the blessed offering to the Lord the prayers rising from earth as a perfume; and they know that their persecutors remain unpunished. Why, then, should those who were either their protectors or the objects of their care here below, and who are now their companions in glory, be alone unrecognized? Why this exception so like a chastisement, this impoverishment of the heart, depriving it of some of its holiest affections, to which, perhaps, too, it owes its entrance into the fatherland of charity, or, at least, a more elevated rank in the kingdom of pure light and perfect love.

[22] St. Gregory Nazianzen, Oration 24, no. 19.

In Heaven We'll Meet Again

It is not necessary for the Christian to pass the waters of oblivion to attain eternal repose. The saint in heaven never loses the recollection of the smallest of his triumphs, nor of the most obscure of his merits. That left hand, which at present knows not what the right hand does (Matt. 6:3), will know it and eternally rejoice in it in heaven. Here below we die to ourselves, by a forgetfulness that is always on the increase as we advance in virtue; but in heaven we shall rise again to ourselves by the most perfect recollection. All the good we shall have effected will revive in our memory with a freshness and brilliancy that we shall never have known. We shall preserve the remembrance of our inward and spiritual trials, as well as that of our physical sufferings and of all our labors. How sweet will it be to us then, in thought, to go over all the furrows of time, when the tears of our eyes and the sweat of our limbs fell like a fertilizing dew to enrich the harvest of our eternal merits!

But could it be that all the happy inhabitants of paradise, in their confidential intercourse, would never speak of their past, would leave the greatness and the multitude of their combats on earth unknown, and would not reveal, one to the other, a single circumstance that would tell that here below they were contemporaries, neighbors, relations, friends? Impossible!

Heaven Is Love and Light

Now, in heaven, with wisdom grows charity, for, as the sun sends us, in one and the same ray, two things together—light and heat—so this mutual recognition that God gives to His elect is always accompanied by love. And as the nearer the flame, the greater the warmth, so the closer we draw to that great God who is a consuming fire (Deut. 4:24), the more are we loved, the more do we love.

Charity never falls away, the Apostle has said (1 Cor. 13:8); and that charity that does not die embraces in its unity God, ourselves, and our neighbor. There are not, in fact, two or three virtues of charity, but only one. If, then, the charity of the just man who dies goes up to heaven with him—if it shines with a more dazzling light on the cloudless horizon of the blessed eternity like a star that, as it rises, increases in splendor, why should that just man cease to burn with the same fire for all those whom he loved with a holy love on earth? Why, when he loves his God more, when he loves himself, shall he not love his neighbor with increased affection?

The holy abbot of Clairvaux mourned his brother Gerard with wondrous tenderness. One of his sermons on the *Canticle of Canticles* is not much else than the funeral oration of this beloved brother. What does he there say? Listen and receive consolation:

The more we are united to God, the fuller we are of love. Now, if God cannot know anguish Himself, He can and does commiserate ours; for to pity the wretched and to pardon the guilty is a thing peculiar to Him. You must, then, brother, be alive to the sufferings of others, since you are intimately united to divine mercy. Therefore your affection for us, far from being diminished, has doubtless attained perfection, and in putting on God you have not laid aside your solicitude for us, since He Himself hath care of us (1 Pet. 5:7), you will have rejected that which was weakness but not that which was tenderness or compassion. In fine, since "charity never falleth away" (1 Cor. 13:8), you will never forget me.[23]

The Angelic Doctor, St. Thomas Aquinas (1225-1274), teaches that the blessed love one another so much the more as they are the more united to God. While on earth we love one another more or less accordingly as we are more or less united with one another by the different ties that are necessary or permitted. However, although we

[23] St. Bernard, *Sermon on the Song of Songs*, 26, no. 3.

Heaven Is Love and Light

St. Thomas Aquinas, *by Carlo Crivelli*

have not to provide in heaven for each other's wants, every soul will retain particular affection for those who were united to it on earth and will continue to love them in several ways—on account of relationship, of friendship, of connection, of benefits granted or received, of compatriotism, or of similarity of vocation. For no motive of honorable love will cease to act upon the heart of one admitted to the joys of heaven.[24]

God Himself told St. Catherine of Siena (1347-1380):

> Though all my elect are indissolubly united together by a perfect charity, there is, nevertheless, a singular communication, a joyous and holy familiarity between those who have mutually loved in this world. Through this mutual love they endeavored to grow in my grace, advancing from virtue to virtue; by it, one was to the other a means of salvation; by it, they helped one another to glorify me in themselves and in their neighbor. This love, therefore, is not in any degree diminished between them in the life everlasting; on the contrary, it brings them a greater abundance of spiritual joy and content.[25]

Without this admirable harmony of knowledge and love, heaven would be devoid of joy. If you light in it only the lamp of knowledge and not the flames of charity,

[24] St. Thomas Aquinas, *Summa Theologica*, II-II, q. 26, art. 13.

[25] St. Catherine of Siena, *The Dialogue*, chap. 41.

jealousies will spread their snares as here below. Think of love in heaven as of a sightless man rushing in his darkness in pursuit of an object, and it will soon prove itself a prey to the gloomiest regrets. Without *love*, nothing would counterbalance inequality; for the soul would cease to possess in others that which was wanting to itself. Without *light*, there would be no consolation for the unhappy end of a beloved being, faithless to his assignation because blind both to the sweet ways of an amiable Providence and to the decrees of eternal justice.

But to unite the perfection of wisdom and the perfection of love is to exclude from heaven selfish jealousies and sour repinings.

The saints enjoy the gifts they possess and do not crave those denied to them. Such even as passed a part of their lives in sin do not the less, for that reason, enjoy unmixed happiness, although they may, perhaps, be less elevated than others in glory.

The great bishop of Hippo said to virgins: "The multitude who will see you follow the Lamb without being able to accompany you will not be jealous. While sharing your rejoicing, they will have in you what they have not in themselves. No doubt, they cannot sing that new canticle (Apoc. 14:3 [RSV = Rev. 14:3]) peculiarly your own; but they can hear it and rejoice in your immense happiness."[26]

He said again: "In the blessed city, none of those who are lower will envy those who are higher, just as now the angels do not envy the archangels. No one wishes to be that which God has not made him, any more than in our body the eye covets the favor of being the finger. To whomsoever God has given lesser gifts, He adds the gift of not wishing for more."[27]

If it is distasteful to you to consult on this matter the too-serious books of the Doctors, take the *Divine Comedy* and read a page of that poem, only the more pleasing to you because a large proportion of it is devoted to theology. In his charming journey to paradise, the author asked a soul he met on its lowest step if it did not desire to rise higher, in order to see and to love more.

"Brother," replied the soul, "there is a virtue in charity which appeases our desires, and, causing us to desire only that which we have, prevents our thirsting for aught else. It is even necessary to our beatific existence to keep

---

[26] St. Augustine, *On Holy Virginity*, 29.
[27] *The City of God*, bk. 22, chap. 30, no. 2.

ourselves to the Divine will, so that all our wills shall form but one. And although in the mansions of our Father we be housed at different stages, the arrangement is one that pleases all in the kingdom, as it pleases the King, who absorbs our will in His. In His will is our peace. His will is that sea towards which take their course both things created and those effected by nature."

"It was then clear to me," concludes the poet, "how every place in heaven is paradise, though the grace of supreme good is not showered down everywhere alike."[28]

Heaven is light.

Since the perfection that renders a created being pleasing to us is found in its plenitude in God, shall we turn our eyes from the focus of eternal splendors, the ocean of infinite perfections, to fix them upon an isolated ray, a slender stream?

The blessed never need turn their looks away from the Creator to observe a creature. It is in Him, it is in the Word that they will contemplate, at the same time, the luminous focus and the rays, the prolific source and the streams. The author of *The Life of the Predestined* wrote:

[28] Dante, *Paradise*, canto 3.

It is in the Divine Word that we shall see truth unadorned, divested of those veils which here never leave us a clear view of all its parts. There will then remain no more doubt in heaven, no more uncertainty, no more shade, no more twilight, and no more utter darkness.

It is in the Word that the predestined will behold, as in an admirable mirror, that great scene of the world unfolding itself in the particular account of every transaction. It is there that he will learn the consequences of the eternal counsels of God in the interests of His own glory. We shall there discern in one view the past, the present, and the future, and we shall walk by the light of this view in the broad paths of eternity, without wandering from the direct way and losing ourselves. We shall there read the universal record of all times, and of the extraordinary events of each succeeding age, not merely in the exterior world, but also in that inward world concealed in the depths of the human heart. It is in this book, then to be opened to the elect, that we shall have the satisfaction of studying the secret history of the heavenly Jerusalem, containing the mystery of the salvation of each *predestined*, and

the particulars of the conduct of God towards men
in the admirable design of their predestination.[29]

Heaven is love.

Do not, therefore, say that there is no further need of
friends — that the saints in ecstasy forget even their relations; and that besides, the greater part of our affections
have their source in a purely natural cause that no longer
exists in eternity. That's a poor philosophy that confines
the sentiments of the heart within the limits of present
utility and comprehends not that the principal benefit of
friendship is the love itself or the intercourse established
between two persons sincerely attached to one another!
How many wise monarchs have considered themselves
happier in possessing a friend than a kingdom!

I do not deny that the saints, in certain moments of
spiritual consolation, and chiefly in ecstasy or ravishment,
have banished all thought of their nearest relations and of
the most virtuous persons: I do not deny that they have
lost all feeling for any but God. But they were on the earth
and in the midst of trial; they were painfully performing
the Master's precept according to the first words of the

[29] Father Rapier, *The Life of the Predestined in the Blessed
Eternity*, chap. 5.

text, "Leave house, brethren, sisters, father, mother, wife, children, lands, for my name's sake"; they had not yet seen the fulfillment of the prophecy contained in the second part—"and receive a hundredfold, and possess life everlasting" (Matt. 19:29).

Heaven is not a forced and transitory state, nor one of ecstasy; it is the permanent city where we have no longer either mortifications to practice nor sacrifices to make in order to mount higher, but where we find in God all that we had left for God. He is the end of our journey and of our combats, and in Him we repose in the tranquil possession of an eternal reward. There the Lord lavishes on all the light that He denies to His greatest servants on earth; and there He gives to charity for our neighbor a liberty of expansion that Christian or cloistral prudence must often restrain in this world. Everything that is good in nature will always exist. Nature will be for glory in heaven what it is here for grace—the necessary foundation. She is a wild plant, but grace is inserted into her like a divine graft. This graft produces, first, flowers tinted with the colors of Jesus Christ and shedding His sweet odor during time. She next produces those fruits of salvation that will be the glory of the blessed throughout eternity. The wild stock with the graft, the entire tree with its fruit, will be transplanted into heaven. We shall even have, in addition to all the faculties of our soul, all the senses of our body without any deficiency. He who dies a little child will rise again a full-grown man.

You were heard to lament when death laid low one of your daughters, still an infant in the cradle; you will be heard rejoicing and glorifying the Lord when you meet this cherished little one again on a throne near Him, having all at once obtained a maturity without decline, eternally beautiful, eternally young. In taking her to Himself, God has assumed the care of bringing her up. He has educated her Himself. Fear not that He will have left no place in her heart for you. On earth, she could neither know nor love you; but in heaven, on account of that first natural connection, God will enable her to know her mother and will give her filial piety as a supernatural virtue.

Heaven is love and light.

Say not, then, "Immense will be the affliction of a saint at the thought of a relation or a friend who never will join him."

From the heights of glory we shall better perceive the horror of sin, the obstinacy of the sinner, and the justice of his condemnation. God, the Sun of the moral world, is the center whose attraction, freely accepted, keeps our souls in the orbit of salvation, in spite of the passions ever stimulating us to diverge. The saints witness with attention, from the eternal hills, the vicissitudes of this struggle, which is to lead those whom they love to heaven or to hell. They long to see that divine attraction, itself the very power of mercy, acting upon the sinner and subduing his insensate or guilty resistance. But, at length, they see that obstinate prodigal, that man who crucifies Jesus a second time, voluntarily yield to the allurement of sin, to the impulse of passion, and altogether quit the orbit of salvation. Like a shattered star cast into space, it wanders farther and farther from its center and thus reaches, through perdition, an infinite distance from God. Now, the affection of the blessed for the souls on earth is weakened in proportion to their separation from the Sovereign Good; and for those who are lost, it becomes totally extinct. Besides, they will what God wills, for they love only what He Himself loves. This is why the Lord said to a great saint:

> The inhabitants of heaven have their desires fully accomplished and are never at variance with me. Their free will is so bound by charity that they cannot desire anything but what I have desired. Their will is so conformed and united to mine, that the father and mother who behold their children in

hell, that the children who behold their father and mother delivered over to eternal sufferings, grieve not at that sight. They even rejoice in seeing those parents or those children punished by my justice who persisted in being my enemies.[30]

But, madam, I think I hear you repeat to me what you have so often said: "How can we console ourselves in *this world* for the misfortune of seeing a beloved person die without any apparent reconciliation with God?"

This question goes a little out of my subject; yet I will not leave it unanswered. I shall, therefore, add a few pages.

[30] Ansaldi, *Della Speranza e della Consolazione di Rivedere i Cari Nostri nell' Altra Vita*, chap. 18.

Let Us Pray for Sinners
Even After Their Unhappy Death

Madam,

The Church condemns none to eternal torments. She publishes decrees to declare that one man is in heaven; she has never published any to declare that another is in hell.

I am happy to know that in reading a work of a deservedly high reputation you particularly remarked these lines:

The Rev. Father de Ravignan (1795-1858) loved to speak of those mysteries of grace called into existence, as he believed, at the hour of death. His feeling seems to have been that a great number of sinners are converted at the last moment, and expire reconciled to God. There are in certain deaths hidden mysteries of mercy and strokes of grace, where the eye of man sees only strokes of justice. By a flash of light God sometimes reveals himself to souls whose greatest misfortune was not to have known Him; and the latest breath may be a sigh calling for pardon, understood by Him who hears it, and who sounds the heart.

Marshal Exelmans (1775-1852), who was precipitated into the grave by a fall from his horse, had neglected the practice of religion. He had promised to have recourse to confession but had not time to do so. Nevertheless, on the very day of his death, a person habituated to heavenly communications seemed to hear an inward voice saying: "Who can tell the extent of my mercy? Can anyone fathom the depths of the sea, and calculate the amount of its waters? Much will be forgiven to certain souls that have remained in ignorance of much." How do we explain these strokes of grace? By the value of a soul purchased by the blood of Jesus Christ and by the mercy that knows no limits; by some good work, almsdeed, or prayer of the sinner during life; by the invisible ministry of the guardian angel, ever prompt to act, and ever ready to save his charge; by the preceding prayers of the just on earth and of the saints in heaven; but, more than all, by the intercession of the Virgin Mary; in fine, by the prayers offered up for sinners after their death, even though they may have given no sign of repentance.

It is to the explanation of this last point that I shall here confine myself.

You read with pleasure, in the work I have just mentioned, those lines of the holy religious written to comfort a queen whose son was killed by a fall from his carriage:

Christians beneath a law of hope, no less than one of faith and love, we must unceasingly raise our thoughts from the abyss of our afflictions to the heights of the infinite goodness of our Savior. As long as a single breath of life remains, no barrier is placed between the soul and grace. We must, therefore, always hope, and make humble and persevering intercession to the Lord. We cannot know to what degree it will be acceptable. Great saints and great Doctors have gone very far in speaking of this powerful efficacy of prayers for beloved souls, whatever may have been their end. We shall someday understand these ineffable wonders of the divine mercy, which we must never cease to invoke with the utmost confidence.[31]

[31] P. de Ponlevoy, *Life of Father de Ravignan*, chaps. 10, 21.

Since the Rev. Father de Ravignan appeals to the saints and the Doctors, I will produce for you the testimony of one who was both a great Doctor and a great saint.

The most eloquent of the archbishops of Constantinople, while arguing to prove that we must not mourn our dead with excess, but rather aid them by our prayers and works, imagines that one of his audience interrupts him, exclaiming: "But I mourn this dear deceased because he died a sinner." What is the reply of St. John Chrysostom?

Is not this a vain pretext? For if such be the cause of your tears, why did you not make more effort to convert him while he lived? And if he really died a sinner, ought you not to rejoice that he can now no more increase the number of his sins?

You must, in the first place, go to his help, as far as you are able, not with tears, but with prayers, supplications, alms, and sacrifices. All these things are indeed not idle inventions. It is not without necessity that in the divine mysteries we commemorate the dead; it is not fruitlessly that we approach the altar with prayers for them to the Lamb who takes away the sins of the world; but by these means is consolation showered upon their souls. If Job could purify his children by offering sacrifice for them, how much more must He whom we offer up for our dead give them relief?

Is it not one of God's ways to do good to some out of regard for others? Let us, then, show ourselves eager to aid our dear deceased and earnestly and perseveringly pray for them. The Mass is a general expiation by which all may profit. In the Mass, therefore, we pray for the whole universe, and we mention the dead with the martyrs, confessors, and priests of the Church; for we are all one body, though some members are more illustrious than others. It may be that we can even obtain for our deceased a complete pardon through the prayers and the merits offered for them by those in whose company they are named. Why, then, are you still in such grief? Why this despondency, these lamentations? May not so great a grace be obtained for him whom you have lost?[32]

We find, in the celebrated revelations of St. Gertrude (1256-c. 1302), an example confirmatory of this doctrine and placing it in a new light. A person had been informed

[32] St. John Chrysostom, *Homily 41 on 1 Corinthians*.

of the death of one of her relations in Gertrude's presence. This person, fearing that the deceased had not died in a state of grace, showed very great affliction. She experienced such trouble as to excite the emotion of the saint, who proposed to pray to God for the departed soul.

She began by saying to our Lord: "Thou couldst have inspired me with the thought and granted me the grace to pray for this soul, without being compelled to do so by tenderness or compassion."

Jesus answered: "I take singular pleasure in the prayers addressed to me for the dead, when natural feeling is added to the goodwill that renders them meritorious, and when both concur to give this work of mercy all the plenitude and perfection it is capable of receiving."

The abbess having afterward prayed long for this soul, became aware of its lamentable state; for it appeared to her frightfully deformed, as black as coal, and resembling a body writhing with intense pain. No spirits were, however, to be seen tormenting it; but evidently its former sins were acting as its executioners.

"Lord," exclaimed the charitable religious, "wilt Thou not be propitiated by my prayers and pardon this man?"

"I would, for the love of thee," replied the Divine Savior, "have pity not only on this soul, but on a million others.

Will thou, then, that I pardon him all his sins, and that I deliver him from every sort of penalty?"

"Perhaps," said the saint, "this may not be in conformity with the requirements of Thy justice."

"It would not be inconsistent with them," added our Savior, "if thou were to ask me for it with confidence. For my divine light, piercing into the future, made known to me that thou would offer this prayer for him. Therefore, I placed good dispositions in his heart, to prepare him for the enjoyment of the fruits of thy charity."[33]

O consoling words! First, by foresight of our future prayers, God deigns to grant good dispositions to the dying sinner that ensure the salvation of his soul; then, in consideration of our present prayers, He consents to deliver this soul from every sort of penalty and to withdraw it from the expiatory flames of purgatory.

The last acknowledgment of the Savior to his virginal spouse is but the particular application of a general principle. Before men could have cast their looks down upon the crib and have raised them to Calvary, before the Sun of Redemption had shone on this lowly vale of our exile, they could already be guided by its light and animated by

[33] *The Insinuations of Divine Piety*, bk. 5, chap. 19.

its heat. Why? Because God the Father, from the summit of the eternal hills, already contemplated the prayers, the sufferings, the virtues, and the merits of His only Son, who was to become incarnate for the salvation of the world.

It is this truth, well understood and carried into practice, that can best render grief productive of virtue. "All my life is now in this," said the person who drew my attention to the above passage in the revelations of St. Gertrude: "Before my husband died, God knew what I should be willing to do for him." She made an entire sacrifice of herself; she consecrated her whole being to the Lord, taking for her motto "Pray, suffer, act"; and the Lord consoled her with the gift of the sick poor of the earth, and the suffering souls of purgatory for her family.

Pray, then, and obtain prayers; God, whose mercy is high and vast as the heavens (Ps. 35:6; 57:6 [RSV = Ps. 36:5; 57:5]), knew at the moment when your friend or your relation was about to die what prayers you would say for him today, tomorrow, and after following the advice contained in this page. Pray, therefore, I repeat, and obtain prayers; your prayers, while consoling and sanctifying you for the present, have already contributed in the past to save those whom you love.

Letter 4

The Family in Heaven

M adam,
You have a particular wish to know what becomes of the family in heaven, if God reconstructs it, and if the hope of enjoying the society of your relations is a consolation in which you may indulge without fear, without scruple, and without imperfection.

Can you doubt it, when so many holy personages assert it by their example as well as by their words?

God has crowned the Christian family with glory and honor, and He causes to shine on its brow the reflection of the three principal mysteries of our religion.

How does it commence?

With a sacrament — the sacred sign of the union of God's word with human nature, of the union of Jesus Christ with the Church, of the very union of God with

the just man. Who has said so? A great pope, Innocent
III (c. 1160-1216).[34]

Then how does it continue? Husbands, love your wives,
as Christ also loved the Church and delivered Himself up
for her; wives, love your husbands, as the Church loves
Jesus Christ and delivers herself up to Him. The great
apostle St. Paul has said it (see Eph. 5:25).

And now you perceive how it ends. By connections
whose origin the angels may envy us, so much do they
recall those of the Trinity, and of such noble joys are they
productive. For man is of man, as God is of God. Who has
said it? A great Doctor, St. Thomas Aquinas.[35]

But could it be that death had more power to destroy
this masterpiece than virtue has the power to preserve
it? And since love is as strong as death (cf. Cant. 8:6
[RSV = Song of Sol. 8:6]), would not the charity of God,
which created the family, would not the charity of man,
which sanctifies its use, reconstruct forever, in heaven,
that which death has destroyed for a time on earth?

Tertullian (c. 155-c. 240) said:

[34] Innocent III, *Prima Collectio Decretalium*, titul. 12, epist. 1.
[35] St. Thomas Aquinas, *Summa Theologica*, I, q. 93, art. 3.

The Family in Heaven

In eternal life God will no more separate those whom He united than He permits their separation in this world below. The wife will belong to her husband, and the husband will still possess the principal thing in marriage, the heart. The want of all carnal tie will be no loss to him. Is not a husband most honored when most pure?[36]

He who gave us this precept: "Let no man separate those whom God hath joined together" (cf. Matt. 19:6) also sets us the example. The Word contracted with humanity a divine marriage. Did He repudiate His spouse when He ascended into heaven? He made her, on the contrary, sit with Him at the right hand of God the Father Almighty. The Man-God has a Mother, blessed among women. Did He disdain to make her share His glory? No; after having associated her with His Passion on earth, He made her take part in the joys of His Resurrection and the glories of His triumph, by assuming her body into heaven after Him, as well as her soul. Jesus Christ had given the name of brother to some men; later did he disown them? Not so; He knew His apostles by the martyrdom they had

---

[36] Tertullian, *On Monogamy*, chap. 10.

The Coronation of the Virgin, *by Fra Angelico*

endured for Him; and in the celestial court He makes Himself known to them by the splendor with which He Himself surrounds them.

But will not the Son of God, who has been pleased thus to reconstruct around Him His family by nature and His family by adoption, in the same way reconstruct, in paradise, that Christian and religious family that belongs to you, and also to Him? He will; and heaven will present a scene not less touching than admirable. As the First Person of the blessed Trinity bending over the Second, says, "Thou art my Son, this day I have begotten thee" (Acts 13:33); and as the Second says to the First with the accents of filial piety, "Father, just Father, holy Father, may those whom thou hast given me be one, as we also are one — I in thee, and thou in me, and I in them" (see John 17:11, 22, 25); so will one human being, bending over another, say with tenderness, "My son, my child, my daughter," and from the heart of the latter will escape this exclamation, "Father!" As the Son of God rejoices that he can say to a woman, "Thou art my Mother," so also will numbers of the elect overflow with rejoicing as they exclaim to a woman, "Mother!"

Now, if it were true that in heaven the members of the same family did not know one another, Jesus would no longer know Mary, or be known by her. Is not this horrible to think and to say? And was not a pious author better inspired who wrote:

> The most holy Virgin preserves all her Mother's authority over the body of her Son, our Lord, even after the Resurrection and Ascension; for her right is inalienable and perpetual. After having taken pleasure during His mortal life in submitting to Mary, Jesus still takes pleasure in showing Himself her Son in the immortal life of the blessed, and in acknowledging her for His Mother. We have the proof of it in those numerous apparitions wherein He has shown Himself in the form of a child in the arms of its mother, and has even given Himself to some saints by her virginal hands. In glory, souls have a continual care of their relations, and particularly of their children, who are a portion of themselves, and, so to say, their second selves. It is, then, an undoubted fact that the Mother of Jesus has her thoughts perfectly fixed on all that concerns the body of her dear Son, in the obscurity of the sacrament as well as in the light of glory. From the heights of heaven, her eyes and her heart follow

Him in every place in which He finds Himself on earth by means of the Eucharistic consecration.[37]

This certainty of a special union with our relations in a blessed eternity is a consolation so pure and so sweet that the saints themselves have made it the subject of their delight. From every point of the compass, from the east, from the west, from the north, from the south, there come voices, bearing testimony to this truth.

Germany offers us among many others the instance of Blessed Henri Suso (c. 1296-1366), a religious of the order of St. Dominic. He was named Henri de Berg, but he preferred the name of Suso, as having been his mother's, in order to do honor to her piety and to be reminded of her without ceasing.[38]

This virtuous mother died on Good Friday, at the same hour as our Lord. Henry was then studying at Cologne. She appeared to him during the night, quite resplendent with glory. "My son," said she, "love Almighty God with all thy strength, and be well convinced that He will never abandon thee in all thy works and difficulties. I have quitted the

[37] De Machault, *Le Trésor des Grands Biens de la Très-Sainte Eucharistie, Nativité de la Très-Sainte Vierge.*

[38] Henri Suso, *Oeuvres du B. Henri Suso.*

world; but this is not to die, since I live happily in paradise, where divine mercy has rewarded the immense love I bore to the Passion of our Savior, Jesus Christ."

"O my holy—O my tender mother!" exclaimed Henri. "Love me ever in heaven as you did on earth, and never abandon me in my afflictions!"

The blessed spirit disappeared; but her son remained, his soul overflowing with consolation.[39]

Another time he saw the soul of his father, who, while living, had had a great love of the world. He appeared to his son in much suffering and affliction, making him thereby understand the excruciating pains he endured in purgatory, and asking for the help of his prayers. Henri shed such burning tears that he soon delivered his father's soul, and it came to thank him for its happiness.[40]

France might, almost as much as Italy, lay claim to the Angelic Doctor. The soul of St. Thomas Aquinas was not dried up by knowledge, but charity kept a prominent place in his heart for his brothers and sisters according to nature.

While he was in Paris, one of his sisters appeared to him to tell him that she was in purgatory. She asked for

[39] Henri Suso, *Life*, no. 39
[40] Ibid., no. 8.

a certain number of Masses, hoping that the goodness of God and the intercession of her brother would deliver her from the flames. The saint asked the students to pray and to offer Masses for the soul of his sister. Afterward, when he was at Rome, she again appeared to him and informed him that she was delivered from purgatory and enjoyed the glory of heaven by virtue of the Masses he had himself said and of those that he had caused to be said.

"And, sister, do you know nothing about me?" exclaimed St. Thomas.

"As for you, brother," replied she, "your life is agreeable to the Lord. You will soon come to meet us; but you will have a diadem of glory more beautiful than ours. Only keep what you have acquired."

"And my brother Landulph, where is he?"

"He is in purgatory."

"And my brother Raynald?"

"He is in paradise, among the martyrs, because he died in the service of the holy Church."[41]

In Spain we meet the illustrious reformer of Carmel, the seraphic Teresa of Jesus (1515-1582). Behind the rails of her convent, in spite of the austerity of her life, she

[41] *Acta Sanctorum, 7, Martii, Vita Sancti Thomae.*

cultivated the purest family affections; and she hoped that God, who gives a hundredfold more to anyone who quits all for His name (Matt. 19:29), would in heaven restore her beloved relations to her a hundredfold, by multiplying her love for them in the same proportion.

One evening Teresa felt herself so ill that she thought she could not meditate, and she had taken her rosary to pray vocally, without any effort of mind. What will our Lord do to console her? She herself informs us in these words: "Some instants had hardly elapsed when a ravishment, with irresistible power, carried me out of myself. I was transported in spirit to heaven, and the first persons whom I saw were my father and mother."[42]

God is pleased to take the heart of the Christian spouse as He took the loaves in the desert (Mark 6:41), to bless and to multiply it, as many times as He gives her children who hunger for His love, and whom she feeds with it, for the glory of the Lord, as well as for her own felicity.

St. Teresa commends a pious lady who, to obtain a family, practiced great devotions and offered fervent prayers to heaven. "To give life to children who, after her death, would praise God, was the petition she presented, without

---

[42] *Life of St. Teresa*, chap. 37.

The Family in Heaven

St. Teresa of Ávila, *by François Gérard*

ceasing, to His divine bounty. Her heart suffered in feeling that, when she would have breathed her last, she would not live again in Christian children and, through them, continue to offer a tribute of blessing and praise to the Lord."

The austere Carmelite says, from herself: "I sometimes think, Lord, that Thou art pleased to grant to those who love Thee the precious favor of providing them, in their children, with fresh means of serving Thee." She says again: "I often reflect on this subject—when these children shall enjoy eternal felicity, and perceive that they owe it to their mother, with what thanksgiving will they not prove their gratitude to her, and with what double joy will not the heart of that mother beat at the sight of their happiness!"

This is what has been thought and said of the family by saints who have remained virgins before, as well as after, their entrance into religious life. Beware, then, of thinking that the child who, from his earliest years, forever consecrates himself to God forgets his father, his mother, his brothers and sisters. On the contrary, his heart becomes the very focus of charity. If this precious treasure were to escape from all other hearts through the breach made by the passions, leaving only indifference and forgetfulness behind, his heart would preserve it and send it unceasingly through the channels of virtue. The oldest, as the youngest, religious is often heard, by his good angel, during the silence of sacrifice and of prayer, saying to the Lord, "Memento, remember my relations who are already dead, and bless them all beyond anything that my heart can desire."

Happy mother, who had it in your power to give two sons and two daughters to Jesus for the glory of His name and the love of His heart! Fear not that those children will be faithless to the Fourth Commandment. The members of religious orders—fruits detached from the bough—are often directed, by their tendency to perfect charity, toward the tree that bore them, to draw upon it honors and benediction. The many benefits, temporal or spiritual, obtained by them from God for their families will never be known till they all meet in heaven.

But I forget: the saints who were not always virgins spoke the same language as the others.

In Africa, behold St. Cyprian, who was reared in paganism and embraced continence only after his baptism. It fell to him, having become bishop of Carthage and destined to martyrdom, to console the faithful threatened with death by an epidemic illness. What said he then? He addressed to them words that the Roman Church recalls to her priests during the octave of the solemn day on which we celebrate all the saints:

> Since we live here below as strangers and travelers, let us sigh for the day that will restore us to our home, and give us back our place in the kingdom of heaven. Who, being in exile, would not long to return to his country? Who, hastening home by sea,

would not desire a favorable breeze to waft him the sooner to the embraces of his dear ones? Heaven is our home, and the patriarchs, our ancestors, are there before us. Let us hasten, then, to see our country and to rejoin our ancestors. Many who are dear to us are expecting us; a considerable number of relations, brothers, children, are anxiously watching for our arrival. They are certain now of their own eternal happiness, and they are full of solicitude for our salvation. To see, to embrace them—what joy both for them and for us![43]

Among the Greeks at Constantinople one of the most intrepid champions of orthodoxy against the iconoclasts of the East, St. Theodore, had first been married; then his wife had, like him, embraced religious life and their children had also entered a monastery.

He wrote to a father whose sons were all dead: "Your children are not lost, but they are safely waiting for you; and as soon as you will have reached the term of this temporal life, you will see them again in joy and blessedness."[44]

---

[43] St. Cyprian, *On Mortality*, 26.
[44] St. Theodore the Studite, *Epistles*, bk. 1, chap. 29.

The Family in Heaven

St. Cyprian, *by the Meister von Meßkirch*

To a widow he wrote:

The God who drew you from nothing to give you existence, the God who brought you to the bloom

St. Theodore Studite, *from Nea Moni Monastery*

of youth to unite you to an illustrious man, will easily unite you to him once more by the resurrection. Look upon his departure, then, as a journey. Would you not resign yourself to it if ordered by a king of earth? Resign yourself to it now, therefore, since you know that He who has ordered this journey is the true King, the sole King of the universe. I exhort you to this; and my hope is that you will meet your husband again in the day of the Lord.[45]

[45] Ibid., bk. 2, *Ad Uxori Demochari.*

The Family in Heaven

And to a man who had just lost his wife he said:

It is to God that you have sent on before so worthy a spouse. Is not this enough for your consolation? And what ought you now to seek? You ought to try to recover in heaven, at the moment fixed by Divine Providence, this excellent companion, who will rejoice with you during ages without end in the participation of ineffable blessings.[46]

No doubt, those who were married on earth, in heaven are like the angels (Matt. 22:30). But although far removed from all the pleasures of sense, they will enjoy forever the purer ones of the spirit and will remember that they were, here below, not only one heart and one soul, like the first Christians (Acts 4:32), but also one flesh, like our first parents (Gen. 2:24; Matt. 19:6).

In Italy, St. Frances of Rome (1384-1440) was married and had children, and when she became a widow she entered religious life.

One morning, toward dawn, the saint had just awakened; she had first raised her heart to God, and next her eyes had fallen on her daughter, still a child, who lay

[46] Ibid, *Ad Nicetae Spathario.*

In Heaven We'll Meet Again

St. Frances of Rome Giving Alms,
by Baciccio (Giovanni Battista Gaulli)

sleeping not far from her. Suddenly her room was filled
with an unusual light, in the midst of which appeared one
of her sons, a year deceased. He was of the same height, the

same figure as when living, but his beauty was incomparably more exquisite. His name was Evangelista. This son, always so loving, approached his mother and saluted her with profound respect and charming grace.

What did Frances then do, transported as she was with unspeakable joy? She did that which every mother would have done: she opened her arms to take this dear child once more to her heart. And what did she say to him? She said, as every mother would have said, "Dost thou, dear son, preserve in heaven the memory of thy mother?"

"O Mother!" answered Evangelista. "See if I think of thee and if I love thee. Dost thou not perceive another child standing near me, whose beauty is superior to mine? He is my companion in the choir of the archangels, for I am in heaven, in the second choir of the inferior hierarchy. This archangel is placed higher in glory than I: nevertheless, God gives him to thee, God leaves him with thee to take my place beside thee, and that of my little sister Agnes, as her soul is soon to flee to paradise and to enter with me into the enjoyment of eternal felicity. This heavenly spirit will console thee in thy pilgrimage, will accompany thee wherever thou goest, and will be found at thy side day and night, so that thou mayest see him with thine own eyes."

This colloquy lasted an hour; and before he departed, the child asked his mother's permission to reascend to heaven, leaving the archangel in her company.[47]

If you have read the life of St. Frances of Rome, given to the public by a noble and zealous Catholic of your own province, you cannot be ignorant of the important part played in the career of this holy woman by the archangel, for whom she was indebted to the prayers of a son who had preceded her to the home of all.[48]

God is always admirable in His saints (Ps. 67:36 [RSV = Ps. 68:35]). The incident now related shows that He is not less so in the delicacy of the consolations with which His heart inundates theirs than in the greatness of the trials and of the miracles He employs to lead them to perfection or to render their sanctity as evident as a burning light. And more: He is not satisfied with consoling them by the joys of the reconstructed family, but He goes further and multiplies their consolation by the charms of friendship transferred to heaven.

---

[47] *Acta Sanctorum*, 11, *Martii, Vita Sanctae Franciscae.*
[48] Vicomte le Bussière, *Vie de Ste. Françoise*, chap. 6.

Letter 5

Friendship in Heaven

Madam,

Beyond the narrow limits of the family, affection may extend within a wide circle of friendship. The Man-God was pleased to have friends on earth, and He has deigned to assemble them around Him in heaven. Following His example, the holiest persons have given free vent to the tenderest feelings of their hearts: all have had friends, chosen out of a thousand, and all have rejoiced in the thought of knowing and loving them in eternal repose.

They have also written admirable pages on true and perfect friendship, a sentiment altogether spiritual. I will merely bring forward one, quite to the purpose. It is by the blessed Ethelred or Aelred (1110-1167), contemporary of St. Bernard, and abbot of the order of Citeaux, in England. It is a conversation between two friends.

ETHELRED. Let us suppose that there is but you in this world, and that all the delights, added to all the riches, of the universe are before you — gold, silver, precious stones, cities surrounded by walls, camps fortified with towers, vast edifices, works of sculpture and of painting. Let us again suppose that you are established in the primitive state, so that all creatures are subject to you as to the first man. Would all these things, I ask, be agreeable to you without a companion?

WALTER. No, assuredly not.

ETHELRED. But what if you had one only companion, whose language, habits, heart, and mind were unknown to you?

WALTER. If I could not obtain from him some sign of friendship, I would rather remain alone than have such a companion.

ETHELRED. But if there were one whom you loved as yourself, and whose affection equaled your own, would not all things before seemingly bitter become at once sweet and pleasant?

WALTER. Quite true.

ETHELRED. In this consists, then, the great and admirable felicity we hope to enjoy in heaven. God will effect between Himself and the creatures whom He will have raised to paradise, between the degrees or the ranks He will have established, between all the elect whom He will have chosen, such great love, such great charity, that each will love all the others as himself. From this mutual love, it will result that every individual soul will rejoice in the felicity of its companions in glory as in its own. The beatitude of each will thus be in common to all, and the total amount of these beatitudes will be the property of each. There no thought will be hidden, no feeling disguised. Such is the true and eternal friendship that commences on earth and is carried on in heaven. It belongs on earth to the few, because the good are few; but in heaven it belongs to all, for all there are good. Here it is necessary to try our friends, as the wise and the foolish are mixed; but on high they need not be tried, since they enjoy an angelic and almost divine perfection. Let us, then, make friends whom we may love as ourselves, who will tell us all their secrets, to whom we shall tell all ours, who will be firm, stable, and constant in all things. For is there, think you, one among mortals who would not thus be loved?

WALTER. I think not.

ETHELRED. If you saw someone living amid numbers of men, and holding them all in suspicion, ever fearing them as if they were disposed to attempt to take his life, loving no one, and believing himself beloved by none, would you not look upon such a man as very unhappy?

WALTER. Yes, as the most unhappy of men.

ETHELRED. You will not, therefore, deny that the happiest is he who abides and reposes in the hearts of those with whom he lives, who loves them all, and is beloved by all, his most sweet tranquillity undiminished by suspicion or by fear.

WALTER. Very good — very true.

ETHELRED. If it be difficult for all to obtain this happiness at present, the future, at least, has it in reserve for us, and in heaven we shall esteem ourselves so much the happier as we shall have had, on earth, a greater number of such friends. Two days ago I was walking around the monastery while the brethren, seated together, formed the most pleasing circle; and, as if I had been in the midst of the delights of paradise, I was admiring the leaves, the flowers, and the fruits of those mystic trees. Not perceiving in that number one whom I did not love, no one of whose love I did not feel assured, my soul was filled to overflowing with a joy so great that it surpassed all the pleasures of this world. I knew that the feelings of my heart stirred in theirs, as did also those of their hearts in mine, and I said with the prophet: "Behold how good and

how pleasant it is for brethren to dwell together in unity"
(Ps. 132:1 [RSV = Ps. 133:1]).[49]

These sentiments of the blessed Ethelred justify the
following words of a more recent author:

Ah! would that I could find expressions sufficiently
tender and strong to describe the sweets of those
chaste and spiritual friendships that will exist in
heaven, where the spirit only will love; and to explain those most holy feelings of tenderness that the
blessed will experience toward one another, with
the loving communications wherein the flesh and
the senses will have no part. What pleasure, what
joy, should I not cause such pure souls as aspire
only to those heavenly affections of which the great
felicity of our future life will be in part composed;
because they will be mingled with the enjoyment
of God Himself, and of the ineffable suavities of
His divine embraces! Are there any delights of the
senses that can deserve to enter into comparison
with these pleasures? If a pure, innocent, sincere,
and faithful friendship often suffices to sweeten the

[49] Aelred, *On Spiritual Friendship*, bk. 3.

whole of this life, what fruit may we not expect to derive from such friendships of the spirit as are to be formed in heaven, accompanied by all these qualities! And, if a safe and faithful friend can make another man most happy even here, what will be the happiness of life everlasting, when all the blessed will be true friends![50]

Now, one of the joys of these true friends will be their mutual recognition. St. Ambrose thought so when he commented on the following words of our Savior: "I have called you friends, because all things whatsoever I have heard of my Father I have made known to you" (John 15:15). By these words our Lord has given the model of friendship for us to copy. We must reveal to our friends all the secrets of our hearts, and we must not remain in ignorance of theirs. A friend conceals nothing. If he is sincere, he opens his mind as our Savior disclosed the mysteries of His Father.[51]

Thus also thought that humble and holy priest of our own days, who was a great prophet without going beyond

[50] Père Rappin, *La Vie des Prédestinez dans la Bienheureuse éternité*, chap. 9.
[51] St. Ambrose, *De Officiis*, bk. 3, chap. 22.

his poor little village, where multitudes visited him living, and visit him still after death. Here are some of his consoling expressions:

> With whom shall we be in heaven? With God, who is our Father; with Jesus Christ, who is our Brother; with the Blessed Virgin, who is our Mother; with the angels and saints, who are our friends. A king, in his last moments, said with deep regret: "Must I then quit my kingdom to go into a country where no one is known to me?" He had never thought of the happiness of heaven. We must make friends there henceforward, in order that we may meet them after death; and then we shall not be afraid, like that king, of not knowing anyone in the other world.[52]

It appears to you, perhaps, that until now I have spoken only of that general friendship that will exist among all the saints in heaven, as it exists on earth, among all the good who know and appreciate each other; and, still more, among all the religious who live in the same community. But does not what I have said apply with greater force to

[52] Alfred Monnin, *Life of the Curé d'Ars*.

a special and holy friendship sometimes seen to blossom during time between two hearts, by virtue of the blood of Jesus Christ?

Firmly believe that such a flower, after having formed your delight on earth, will shed its odors in a blessed eternity, to perfume the celestial court, and to give ever-new consolation to the elect.

The saints even considered the possibility of such persistence as an essential of friendship. Who does not know that saying of St. Jerome, "The friendship was never true that can have an end"?[53] The friendship that cannot be eternal has no real existence, and true friendship survives all separations of death, to reunite in heaven those whom she unites on earth.

You have read those lines of St. Francis de Sales (1567-1622) describing true friendship as the prelude and foretaste of heaven:

If your reciprocal communication is made up of charity, of devotion, of Christian perfection, O God! How precious will your friendship be! It will be excellent, because it came from God; excellent,

[53] St. Jerome to Ruffin, *Selected Letters*.

St. Francis de Sales

because it tends to God; excellent, because its bond is God; excellent, because it will last forever in God. Oh! How pleasant it is to love on earth as they love in heaven and to learn mutually to cherish one another in this world as we shall do throughout eternity in the next! The delicious balm of devotion distills from heart to heart by continual participation; and so it may be said that God has extended His blessings and the life of ages upon ages over such friendship. Never did so chaste a tie change but into a union of spirits more perfect and more pure — a living image of the blessed friendships to exist in heaven.[54]

Feel no scruple, then, when death deprives you of a friend, in consoling yourself by repeating: "She forgets me not? She prays for me, she watches over me; we remain united."

Thus did St. Gregory Nazianzen console himself after the death of St. Basil, his perfect friend: "Now," said he, "Basil is in heaven. It is there he offers his former sacrifices for us, and breathes forth fresh prayers for the people; for in departing he has not altogether left us. At times even he comes to warn me by nocturnal visions, and he reproves me when I deviate from my duty."[55]

In this manner St. Augustine likewise consoled himself when death had carried away one of his friends to Abraham's bosom. "It is there," exclaimed he, "that my Nebridius is living — my sweet friend, thy adopted child, O Lord! It is there he lives, there he drinks in all the wisdom for which he thirsts. Still, he is not, I think, so inebriated with it as to forget me. How could he forget me, since thou

[54] St. Francis de Sales, *Introduction to the Devout Life*, pt. 3, chaps. 19, 20.
[55] St. Gregory Nazianzen, *Oration* 43, no. 80.

St. Gregory Nazianzen, *fresco from Kanye Cami, Istanbul*

thyself, Lord, who art the draught of wisdom to my friend, rememberest us?"[56]

A holy bishop, writing to a holy pope, affords us another instance of the same views. In anticipation of death,

---

[56] St. Augustine, *Confessions*, bk. 9, chap. 3, no. 3.

whose strokes could not long fail to fall on both, he thus seeks comfort:

> Let us, at all times and in all places, remember and pray for one another; let us strive to soften our pains and anguish by our mutual love; and if one of us, through the goodness of God, precede the other to heaven, may our friendship continue in the presence of God, and our prayers unceasingly implore the mercy of our Father in favor of our brothers and sisters.[57]

You may go still further. After having previously consoled yourself to a certain degree by a strong hope that your friend would pray more efficaciously for you if she were the first to reach heaven, you will rejoice in the thought of rejoining her there, and you will say to her: "In paradise we shall be together—yes, together in the presence of God; and there how much more dearly shall we love one another!"

But some may be found who will endeavor forcibly to repress all these sentiments of a loving heart and who will make you this reproach: "What! Is it not a manifest and

[57] St. Cyprian to Cornelius, *Letters*, 60.

gross imperfection to rouse your courage and to stimulate
yourself in your struggle with the world, by the hope of
reposing on the bosom of those whom you love?" You may
reply, madam, that there have been great saints who were
even more sensible than you to this hope and that they
desired to enjoy again, in a blessed eternity, the chaste
embraces of their friends.

The Apostle of India acknowledged this to the founder
of the Society of Jesus. St. Francis Xavier (1506-1552)
wrote to St. Ignatius:

> You say in the excess of your friendship for me, that
> you would most ardently wish to see me once more
> before you die. Oh! God alone, who looks into the
> heart, knows how vivid and how deep an impres-
> sion this dear proof of your affection has made on
> my soul. Each time I recall it—and that happens
> often—my eyes involuntarily fill with tears; and if
> the delightful idea that I could embrace you once
> more presents itself to my mind (for, however dif-
> ficult it might appear at first sight, there is nothing
> that holy obedience cannot accomplish), I find
> myself for an instant surprised by a torrent of tears
> that no power can arrest.

St. Francis Xavier, *by Joseph Vien*

I pray God that if we are not to see each other again while living, we may together enjoy in a happy eternity the repose never to be found in this life.[58]

It is all over; we never shall meet again on earth otherwise than by letters; but in heaven—ah! We shall meet face-to-face. And then with what transport shall we not embrace one another![59]

Who, indeed, can tell the transports which two virtuous friends will experience for each other eternally in heaven, after having here below loved each other unto perfection, and verified the saying of Holy Scripture: "A faithful friend is the medicine of life and immortality; and they that fear the Lord shall find such a friend" (Sir. 6:16)?

[58] *Letters of St. Francis Xavier*, Letter 42.
[59] Ibid., Letter 2.

Letter 6

The Union of Men and
Angels in Heaven

Madam,

God Almighty, not content to grant us primary beatitude—the vision of Uncreated Good (that is, of Himself)—denies us not, besides, that part of secondary beatitude consisting of the knowledge and love of our friends and relations. Far from it, He will even multiply joys and pleasures for the eyes, the tongue, the taste, the smell, and the touch—in a word, for all the senses of the body.[60] He will "renew the heavens and the earth" (cf. Apoc. 21:1 [RSV = Rev. 21:1]), that through our senses, as well as through our intellects, we may derive enjoyment from beings devoid of reason.

[60] Robert Bellarmine, *On the Eternal Happiness of the Saints*, bk. 4, chap. 5; Drexelius, *Reflections on Eternity*, bk. 2.

"If bodies," says St. Thomas, "have merited nothing of themselves, man has done so for them; he has merited that glory should be given them, to increase his own glory. Thus, when anyone has acquired a new dignity, it is just that he should assume more sumptuous attire, to correspond with his fresh glories."

St. John Chrysostom employs two other comparisons:

When a royal prince takes possession of the paternal throne, does not the nurse who reared him receive many additional gifts and favors? Well! Material creatures are our nurses. When a son is to appear in public invested with some high office, does not the father, in order to do him honor, take care to bestow richer garments upon his servants? So will our heavenly Father, when he presents us in the world on high with the white toga of manhood, with the rightful insignia of our rank, increase our glory by robing with incorruptibility those material works of His creation which are our servants.[61]

If so, then, how much more must the saints, both before and after the blessed resurrection, enjoy those pure

---

[61] St. John Chrysostom, *Homily 14 on Romans*.

spirits who range above other creatures, and with whom, through our souls, we have a real affinity! Already we love and honor them; in heaven we shall also see them, and we shall each of us know our own benign guardian. There we shall be placed among the angelic choirs, in a rank determined by the degree of our merits or by the nature of our virtues.[62]

St. Thomas thinks that some blessed souls are already enthroned in the highest ranks of celestial spirits, and that in a position so elevated they have a clearer view of God than the inferior angels.[63]

Not an angelic choir will be excepted; in all, sooner or later, the thrones left vacant by the fallen spirits will be seen filled by men.

St. Bonaventure shares this opinion and thinks that the blessed whose merit does not attain the level of the least exalted of the angels form a tenth order or choir.[64] In this order, no doubt, are to be found infants who,

---

[62] Potho (Presbyter Prumiensis), *De Statu domus Dei libri quinque*, bk. 4, chap. 14; De Barry, *La Dévotion aux Anges*, chap. 3; St. Catherine of Siena, *The Dialogue*, chap. 12.

[63] St. Thomas Aquinas, *Summa Theologica*, I-II, q. 4, art. 5, ad. 6.

[64] St. Bonaventure, *Sentences*, bk. 2, dist. 9, art. 1, q. 7.

St. Bonaventure, *by Claude François*

forestalled by death, could add no personal merit to the grace of their baptism—blessed angels, whom their mothers invoke as consolation for no longer beholding them, and who have become the zealous patrons of their families. Of how great an evil, then, are those women guilty who shrink from the pains of childbirth or shun the troubles of education; and of what joys do they deprive themselves forever by avoiding to people heaven with little angels, who, at their entrance into glory, would advance to greet them, and who would encircle them eternally with homage! As for you, madam, happier far, you will see your numerous children, your relations, and all whom you most loved on earth, swell the ranks of the angels, and form, perhaps, the greatest ornament of their respective choirs. May this hope be your solace, as it has already proved that of a mother afflicted, like you, by the death of more than one child!

St. Frances of Rome, in a vision, saw several blessed souls ascending to take their places in eternal glory according to the rank assigned them by God. All the angelic choirs through which these souls passed, as they rose higher and higher, lavished on them the sincerest proofs of love and the liveliest signs of joy. It is ever thus. But the choir wherein the newly arrived soul occupies a throne surpasses all the others in thrilling congratulations and in transports of bliss. In it is intoned a canticle of praise and thanksgiving in honor of the God of all goodness, and in it this sweet rejoicing continues long after it has ceased to resound in the other choirs.

Since having that vision, every time the saint strove to express the joy of the angels on the arrival of the souls of the blessed in heaven, and the admirable union of human and angelic creatures, her face became crimson, and she seemed to melt like wax before the fire.[65]

With what joy must have been welcomed, and to what heights must have ascended, your daughter who bore the name of the Queen of Angels and who was herself an angel of piety, of devotedness, and of purity! She daily sought your blessing, and at sight of her portrait your hand still, as if by instinct, moves to bless her. Now, however, it is she who, each day, sends down from on high the blessings she implores for you from God—all those most desired by the saints, blessings of suffering and crosses, and, with them, blessings of patience and love. Rejoice, therefore, in her happiness; it must constitute yours, for Mary is more in her place in heaven than on earth, amid angels than men.

The suavity of this holy union, contracted in the homeland of spirits, between angels and men, has been described to us by the genius of some of our great Catholic authors.

St. Thomas Aquinas gives us to understand that the angels place part of their felicity in reigning, each, with the blessed one who was confided to his care; in sitting on the same throne; in wearing, so to say, the same crown; and in forming with him but one heart and one soul; since

[65] *Acta Sanctorum, 11, Martii, Vita Sanctae Franciscae.*

every man is to have in heaven an angel to reign with him or in hell a demon to torture him.[66]

St. Bonaventure tells us that the beatitude of man, his former charge, increases the joy of the angel, both as to extension, since he has the felicity of another to share, and even as to intensity. This intensity is not, it is true, to be understood as applying to the primary, but merely to the secondary reward. It may be explained by the increased good of the angels themselves, by the good of the sanctified creatures whom they tenderly love, and especially, in each case, by the good of the soul that was, in particular, the most intimately connected with an angel, because the latter was the minister of its salvation and performed for its sake a thousand beneficent actions. All this is to the angels a source of rejoicing and of congratulation.[67]

Between the guardian angel and the blessed object of his care will occur mysteries of love, to be neither seen nor understood by us until the mists of earth shall have been dispersed by the radiance of heaven. The spirit lays before the man the affecting view of all his efforts to keep him in the right path and to lead him to perfection and unfolds

[66] St. Thomas Aquinas, *Summa Theologica*, I, q. 113, art 4.
[67] St. Bonaventure, *Sentences*, bk. 2, dist. 11, art. 2, q. 2.

to him the whole plan of Divine Providence in the work of his salvation. The saint replies to the heavenly spirit by testifying his gratitude a thousand times over, by recalling the confidence with which he used to recommend himself to his good angel, by assuring him that the happy past is ever fresh in his memory and that these recollections are as perfumes to his soul, still inhaled with delight, even amid the joys of paradise.

Often in this endearing converse, the angel and the man draw closer together, impelled by that divine breath called the charity of patriotism; and from one heart into the other fall the effusions of a penetrating joy, like unto the dew of heaven.

Thus, in the gardens of earth, we sometimes see two neighboring flowers bowed down till they meet by the action of a favoring breeze, as if to give the kiss of peace, and to mingle their treasures together.

The great poet who has so admirably described paradise is, therefore, again in the right. On one hand, he shows that men know each other in heaven, even when they have not been acquainted on earth.

St. Thomas recognized his master, Albert the Great; but he also knew Denis the Areopagite, Bede, and Isidore. St. Bennet recognized his disciples; and the prince of

The Union of Men and Angels in Heaven

Dante and Beatrice with Thomas Aquinas, Albertus Magnus, Peter
Lombard and Siger of Brabant, *by Philipp Veit*

the apostles recognized St. James; but the great abbot of
Clairvaux also knew the father of all mankind, and the
father of the Church, Simon Peter, St. Augustine, and a
crowd of others, whom he could not have known here

below. Furthermore, angels and men know each other. St. Bernard knows the Archangel Gabriel, and all the pure spirits know the incomparable Virgin, who is the Mother of God.[68]

At times, this powerful genius imagines heaven to be like a garden, through which flows a stream of light of dazzling splendor, between two banks tinted with the colors of a wondrous spring. From this stream of light issue bright sparks, flying from all parts to rest on the flowers, like rubies set in gold. Then, as if inebriated with perfumes, they fly back to their brilliant source, and as one enters, another departs. These sparks are angels — these flowers are saints.

At other times, he represents paradise as a white rose, exhaling a perfume of praise to the sun, which engenders perpetual spring. For, since the blessed from earth are ranged in circles on more than a thousand steps, and the circles widen as the steps rise higher, this arrangement reminds him of the form of the rose, whose petals increase in size as they recede from the center, in which the yellow stamens bloom. "This is why," said he, "the heavenly host, espoused by Christ in His blood, showed itself to me in the form of a white rose."

[68] Dante, *Paradise*, cantos 10, 22, 23, 25, 32.

The Union of Men and Angels in Heaven

But the angels who, while flying, ceased not to see and to sing the glory of their Creator, had golden wings and faces beaming with light; the rest of their bodies was whiter than snow. On whatever step they might happen to alight, there they brought the glow of love and shed the fragrance of peace. First, they flew down into the great flower adorned with so many leaves; then they rose up to the perpetual abode of their love, that is, toward the heart of God, like a swarm of bees, sometimes settling on the flowers, and at others returning to the place whence the savor of their work proceeds.[69]

Madam, you may fearlessly have recourse to these poetic images to represent to yourself the blessed company of angels and of men. When heaven is in question, or the happiness of the elect, no images borrowed from earth can exaggerate, but they rather fall far short of the reality. For, here below, "eye hath not seen, nor ear heard, neither hath it entered into the heart of man, what things God hath prepared for them that love him" (1 Cor. 2:9).

Besides, did not our Lord Himself borrow an image from earth to give us an idea of heaven when He compared it to a banquet (see Matt. 8:11; Luke 13:29)? As

[69] Ibid., cantos 30, 31.

the seven sons of Job invited one another in turn, each on his day, to a splendid feast (Job 1:4), so in paradise the children of God bid each other to the partaking of their felicities. Great must have been the reciprocal love of Job's sons when they placed all their riches in common; but how much is fraternal love exceeded by the mutual love of the angels and saints! How much more abundant and inexhaustible are the riches of God than those of Job! How far does the number of the children of God in heaven surpass that of the most prolific parents on earth! What, then, is the magnificence of the banquet to which each of the choirs of angels is summoned by each of the choirs of saints, who have gone up from the valley of exile to the eternal hills of the homeland!

Fair heaven, delicious banquet, where the seraphim and the cherubim send around as a precious liquor and a life-giving manna the manifestation of divine secrets, the clearness of their contemplations, the ardor and the activity of their charity — where the thrones, the dominations, the principalities, the powers, the virtues, the archangels, the angels, and men, patriarchs, prophets, apostles, martyrs, pontiffs, confessors, and virgins, pour out their beings, in turn, into one another's hearts, as into an enchanted cup, ever overflowing, and yet ever full of that which it has given — the wine of God, the wine of knowledge and of purity, the wine of gratitude and of joy!

Thus, in the heights of heaven, under the eyes of the Father of the family, all His children — those who are pure spirits and those who are covered with a veil of flesh — know, esteem, and love one another and converse together in a perfect communication, a constant interchange of glory, of felicity, of light and of love. All those stars, shining in the firmament of eternity without any fear of eclipse, cross their rays and their fires, reciprocally inundate each other with their brightness, and seem to float in an ocean of ineffable splendor; all those animated instruments that never cease to resound under the impulse of divine love, form a sea of harmony, where billow mingles with billow, the strongest of them giving of its abundance to the weakest, in order that their movements, like regulated and irresistible waves, may encroach upon and carry away all things toward God.

Letter 7

The Benefits of Remembering
Our Departed Loved Ones

Madam,

All that I have written, so far, ought not to make you forget that the essence of beatitude is the clear vision or the intuition of God Himself. The knowledge of creatures added to the knowledge of the Creator appears to the blessed less than a drop of water to the ocean. They say with the son of Amos: "All nations, all families of men, angels, and stars, cannot enter into comparison with God alone; they are before him as if they had no being at all, and are counted to him as nothing and vanity" (Isa. 40:15, 17). And with the son of Monica they say:

Lord, God of all truth, how unhappy is the man who knows all creatures and who knows not Thee! How fortunate is he who knows Thee, even if he is learned in naught else! He who unites these two sciences, that of the Creator and that of the creature, finds not his happiness increased by the knowledge of created beings; but Thou alone, O my God, renderest him happy.[70]

It is not for this less true, as I think I have sufficiently proved to you, that a part of the secondary beatitude reserved by the Lord for all His elect consists in the knowledge of creatures.

The inhabitants of heaven know all the mysteries of the past, and feel joy at sights that too often sadden us. A pious and learned cardinal, treating of the eternal felicity of the saints, wrote:

What shall I say of the course of times and of ages, from the commencement to the end? What exquisite enjoyment will not the elect receive in contemplating so many vicissitudes and changes among the things governed with wisdom, and guided to their ends by an inimitable Providence! Have we not here that stream of the river which so marvelously maketh the city of God joyful? (Ps. 45:5). What, in

[70] St. Augustine, *Confessions*, bk. 5, chap. 4.

fact, is it but the order and succession of ages flow-
ing rapidly, and never interrupting their course, if
it be not the impetuosity of a stream unremittingly
rushing toward the ocean, into which it plunges and
disappears? While the stream of time flows on, many
men doubt God's Providence. Among His own servants some are troubled or seriously tempted, and
murmur at His government. For this rapidity of the
stream often causes great damage to the good and
benefit to the wicked, carrying away the soil from
the lands of the just man to deposit it on the fields
of the impious. But when time shall have run its
course, and the stream shall have entered into the
sea, the saints will plainly read in the books of Divine Providence the reasons for all the revolutions
of nature and of history. Then will the impetuosity
of this stream, represented by memory, make joyful
the city of God beyond aught that mortal tongue
can tell.[71]

But in the infinite mirror of the divine essence, wherein
all things are seen, the souls of the blessed principally

[71] Robert Bellarmine, *On the Eternal Happiness of the
Saints*, bk. 4, chap. 4.

discern that which concerns those who are attached to them by the closest ties.[72]

This is, I think, superabundantly proved by all the testimonies I have produced instead of speaking from myself. I have done so that your spirit may be the more surely soothed by thus living for a time in the company, or, better still, in the intimacy, of the saints and of the doctors, whose hearts were ever most tender and most compassionate.

If, then, anyone should presume again to tell you that in heaven we do not recognize one another, show him that "cloud of witnesses" hovering over your head, of whom the Apostle speaks (Heb. 12:1). They are all the learned and virtuous authors whom I have cited to you, and many more whom I might have cited. They form a cloud, as it were, of fire, whose effulgence gives evidence that the Sun of truth has arisen above the earth and gilds it with His rays. They form a cloud whose softness and depth give sweet repose to our eyes, and to our hearts a hope of the fertilizing showers of consolation. Their opponents also form clouds, but dark and lowering ones. They increase the horror of the obscurity in which we live and, with a somber shadow,

---

[72] Jacques-Bénigne Bossuet, *Sermon pour la Profession d'une Demoiselle que la Reine Mère avait Tendrement Aimée.*

intercept our view of the eternal light to which we look forward. They shut out from our knowledge and love those brilliant stars called the blessed in heaven and force our looks to settle sadly on the tomb when we most need to raise them to heaven, in order to find a little light and joy.[73]

To deny that we know our own in heaven is then to do much harm, to increase sorrow, and to turn it into faintness of spirit and despair. But to diffuse the important truth now established is to soften affliction, to sustain piety, and to animate zeal; these are three practical conclusions remaining for me to develop.

Few men have had a soul so sensible to the loss of friends as the amiable François Fénelon, archbishop of Cambrai. Is it not he who has written the following?

> We could be tempted to wish that all good friends might wait to die on the same day. Those who have no affection would bury the whole human race with dry eyes and light hearts; such men are unworthy to live. Our sensibility to friendship costs us much, but those who possess it would be ashamed to be

[73] Ansaldi, *Della Speranza e deIIa Consolazione di Rivedere i Cari Nostri nell' Altra Vita*, chap. 1.

without it — they would rather suffer than be devoid of feeling.[74]

See how, nevertheless, Archbishop Fénelon could set aside his own affliction to console those more afflicted than he. At the death of his friend, the Duke of Beauvilliers, he wrote to the Duchess:

No; only the senses and the imagination have lost their object. He whom we can no longer see is with us more than ever. We find him unceasingly in our common center. He sees us there, he there obtains for us real helps and knows our infirmities better than we do, though now delivered from his own; he also prays for the remedies requisite for our cure. As to me, who had been deprived of seeing him during so many years, I now speak to him, I open my heart to him, I seem to find him in the presence of God; and although I bitterly wept for him, I cannot think that I have lost him. Oh, what reality there is in this intimate association![75]

[74] Cardinal de Bausset, *Histoire de Fénelon, Mort du Duc de Chevreuse*.
[75] *Correspondance de Fénelon*.

The Benefits of Remembering

Fénelon, again, wrote to the widow of the Duke of Chevreuse:

> Let us unite in heart with him whom we regret; he has not been removed far away from us, though he has become invisible. He sees us, he loves us, he is affected by our wants. Having himself arrived safely in port, he prays for us who are still in danger of shipwreck. He says to us in a whisper: "Hasten to join us."
>
> Pure spirits see, hear, and still love their true friends in their common center. Their friendship is immortal, like its source. Unbelievers love themselves only; they must be in despair when they lose their friends, as they think it is forever; but *divine friendship* changes visible company into a company of pure faith; she weeps, but while weeping finds an alleviation to her sorrow in the hope of rejoining her friends in the land of truth and in the bosom of love.[76]

What can be better calculated to maintain piety than these affectionate and confidential relations that may be

[76] Bausset, *Histoire de Fénelon.*

established between us and our dear deceased from the moment we are permitted to hope that, having died in the grace of God, they no more forget us than we forget them? No doubt it is the enjoyment of the presence of the Lord and our communion with Him, even in this mortal life, which does most to nourish our piety. Still, to commune and treat with the saints of heaven long and often, whenever we please, is not this a powerful means at the same time of sanctification and of consolation? By this practice do we not, in some degree, participate in the privilege of the angels, who have continual intercourse and the sweetest familiarity with the saints? The remembrance of a virtuous and faithful friend whom we possess in this world is often enough to drive far from us, besides care and sadness, temptation, despair, and all evil thoughts. How much more efficacious and salutary for our souls, then, must be the thought, the frequentation, sometimes even the conversation of those friends and relations who behold the Lord face-to-face and who are in the enjoyment of His glory!

A pious author, Father de Barry, advises us to invoke those who, although the Church has not held them up publicly to our veneration, led a holy life on earth, or whose end at least was edifying—particularly if their love for us was pleasing to God. He said:

The Benefits of Remembering

Make a list of them, and once a year, or rather once a week, read it over, and invoke those inscribed on it. This habit can only be productive of a more ardent desire to meet again, in heaven, the happy number of those who were united to you on earth. How great will be your bliss when you obtain from God, through their intercession, gifts that you have long solicited in vain. For I do not doubt that by their intervention our prayers are sometimes answered. If they loved us living, and could not find in their hearts to refuse our requests, how will it not be with them now, since their charity has become far more ardent and they are in so much greater favor with God?[77]

St. Francis Xavier often invoked those in the Society of Jesus who had died. He had recourse to all those whom he had known and with whom he had lived; he recommended to them all his undertakings, considered them as his patrons at the celestial court, and declared that he frequently found their prayers of great service.

[77] P. de Barry, *Hagiophili sanctum foedus cum sanctis caeli civibus ineundum*.

St. Louis Bertrand (1526-1581) of the Order of St. Dominic had composed entire litanies with the names of his dearest friends whom he thought already in the possession of eternal happiness, and he often invoked them in his need.

In the *Life of M. Emery, Ninth Superior of the Seminary of St. Sulpice*, we read, on the subject of the former priests of this society who had given the greatest edification by their virtues:

> In several of his retreats he formed the resolution of drawing up, from the burial charts of the seminary, a memorandum to remind him of the days of the decease of such of those holy priests as inspired him with the greatest devotion, in order that he might invoke them on those days with fervor, and return thanks to God for the eminent sanctity to which He had raised them.[78]

There is only one objection that you can make to so pious a practice: "Perhaps my friends and relations are not in heaven — perhaps they are in purgatory." It is true that the Church has not proclaimed where they are. But

[78] Jean Edme Auguste Gosselin, *Vie de M. Emery*, 1, no. 53.

The Benefits of Remembering

St. Catherine of Bologna, *by Guglielmo Giraldi*

prayer never goes astray, and among the great number whom you would thus invoke, some must certainly have reached the haven of felicity. Several grave theologians are of opinion that the souls in purgatory can themselves pray for us, as they are not in a worse condition than the living who are sinners and enemies of God. They are even confirmed in the grace and friendship of the Lord; they possess the perfection of charity; they remember all that they owe us; and they can know of our prayers through their guardian angels. Why should they not, then, pray to God for us, since they come sometimes to pray to us for themselves, as we see in the life of St. Bridget that the soul of her husband appeared to her and prayed to her to have Masses said and alms distributed to the poor?[79]

St. Catherine of Bologna (1413-1463) frequently invoked the souls in purgatory, and said that God had granted her, through their intercession, the greatest and the most numerous favors. "Often even," added she, "that which for a long time I could not obtain through the prayers of the saints in heaven, I have obtained as soon as I had recourse to those suffering souls."[80]

Finally, let the hope of meeting them in heaven, of recognizing them and of being recognized by them, reanimate your zeal and stimulate you to work with greater ardor for the relief of these poor souls, as well as for the conversion of sinners.

[79] *Révelations de Ste. Brigitte*.
[80] *Acta Sanctorum, Vita Sanctae Catherine de Bologna*.

The souls in purgatory are so thankful for all that is done for them that persons who have relieved them receive proofs of their gratitude before they can join them in heaven.

It was even given to St. Gertrude, who had so great a zeal for their deliverance during her life, to see and to converse with those whom she had succored.[81]

One day after Communion Gertrude offered the adorable Host for the repose of the souls of all the deceased relations of the members of the community. She immediately saw a great number of souls like sparks or stars emerge from darkness.

"Lord," exclaimed she, "are there none in this multitude but the souls of our relations?"

"I am, myself," replied the Lord, "your nearest relation; I am your brother, your father, and your spouse. All those who are especially mine thus become your relations and connections, and it is my will that they have a share in the fruits of the prayers offered up by you for your relations."[82]

Continue then, Madam, to pray for your husband, your children, and all the members of your family whom God

[81] *The Insinuations of Divine Piety.*
[82] Ibid.

St. Gertrude, *by Miguel Cabrera*

has withdrawn from this earth. If their souls are, as I hope, already in the place of refreshment, light, and peace, your prayers will relieve others of the household of Jesus Christ and snatch them from the expiatory flames to introduce them into eternal repose.

The Benefits of Remembering

But limit not your zeal to the dead: let it be catholic, or universal, like the Church. Among the living, how many sinners, how many infidels, are there, whose return to God you may hasten by your cares, by your prayers, by your alms, and by all your merits! Have compassion on their misery, for they are blind men, led onward to the ruin of all that is love by the very disorder of their delusive affections. To none so much as to the souls of the lost can St. Paul's description of the heathens be applied: "They are without affection" (cf. Rom. 1:31). If it be true that the original elements of natural affection remain in hell, it is, alas, so far only as they are evil and disunited from Jesus Christ. Moreover, they no longer produce there any but fruits of bitterness — a hatred so much the greater as there seemed the greater love. But in bringing the lost sheep back to the Shepherd, and the prodigal child to his Father, you prepare for yourself in heaven the fulfillment of these words of the prophet:

> Lift up thy eyes round about, and see all these are gathered together; they are come to thee: I live, saith the Lord, thou shalt be clothed with all these as with an ornament, and as a bride thou shalt put them about thee. The children of thy barrenness

shall still say in thy ears: The place is too strait for me, make me room to dwell in. (Isa. 49:18, 20)

To those whom you will have converted, you may say like the Apostle: "My little children, of whom I am in labor again, until Christ be formed in you, my most desired, my joy and my crown" (cf. Gal. 4:19; Phil. 4:1). In view of this crown of joy awaiting you in paradise, when the time shall come to leave this sad place of exile, you will have the comfort of saying to yourself: "I am going to be reunited to those whom I have sent before me to our own country; I am going to see them again and to recognize them, to enjoy the proofs of their gratitude and of their love."

You may even say to those whom you are leaving on earth, as the Master said to His disciples: "I go to prepare a place for you, that where I am you may also be" (cf. John 14:2, 3). "A little while, and now you shall not see me, because I go to the Father. I will see you again, and your heart shall rejoice, and your joy no man shall take from you" (John 16:16, 22).

But the Lord will deign to leave you, madam, yet a long time among us, for the happiness of your children and of your grandchildren, as well as for the edification of all the faithful.

The Benefits of Remembering

Such, at least, is the wish and the prayer, madam, of your most humble and devoted servant.

F. Blot, S.J.
Strasbourg, August 15, 1862
Feast of the Assumption
of the Blessed Virgin Mary

Sophia Institute

Sophia Institute is a nonprofit institution that seeks to nurture the spiritual, moral, and cultural life of souls and to spread the Gospel of Christ in conformity with the authentic teachings of the Roman Catholic Church.

Sophia Institute Press fulfills this mission by offering translations, reprints, and new publications that afford readers a rich source of the enduring wisdom of mankind.

Sophia Institute also operates two popular online Catholic resources: CrisisMagazine.com and CatholicExchange.com.

Crisis Magazine provides insightful cultural analysis that arms readers with the arguments necessary for navigating the ideological and theological minefields of the day. *Catholic Exchange* provides world news from a Catholic perspective as well as daily devotionals and articles that will help you to grow in holiness and live a life consistent with the teachings of the Church.

In 2013, Sophia Institute launched Sophia Institute for Teachers to renew and rebuild Catholic culture through service to Catholic education. With the goal of nurturing the spiritual, moral, and cultural life of souls, and an abiding respect for the role and work of teachers, we strive to provide materials and programs that are at once enlightening to the mind and ennobling to the heart; faithful and complete, as well as useful and practical.

Sophia Institute gratefully recognizes the Solidarity Association for preserving and encouraging the growth of our apostolate over the course of many years. Without their generous and timely support, this book would not be in your hands.

www.SophiaInstitute.com
www.CatholicExchange.com
www.CrisisMagazine.com
www.SophiaInstituteforTeachers.org

Sophia Institute Press® is a registered trademark of Sophia Institute.
Sophia Institute is a tax-exempt institution as defined by the
Internal Revenue Code, Section 501(c)(3). Tax I.D. 22-2548708.